'LOOKING BACK'

at

LILLIPUT

POOLE, DORSET

by

IRIS MORRIS

Old Thyme Publishing

2nd Floor

Jonsen House

43 Commercial Road

Poole, Dorset BH14 OHU

The author has lived in Poole for over 40 years,
and has published two other local history books -

1993 The Llewellin Family of Upton House

1996 'Looking Back'
A Social History of the Village of Ashley Cross in Parkstone

ISBN 0 9520752 2 9

Cover photographs courtesy of:
Front cover - John Dodds Studio
Back Cover - S Sieger, Lilliput W I, Eldridge Pope
Inside covers - Poole Reference Library

Designed and printed by Marquee Print (01202) 769077
www.marqueeprint.com

CONTENTS

INTRODUCTION

The boundaries of Lilliput, as with other areas of Poole in Dorset, are difficult to define. The harbour shore is positive enough from the Blue Lagoon to the Luscombe Valley but the edges of its semi-circle blur into Whitecliff, Parkstone, Canford Cliffs and Sandbanks. However, it is Parkstone from which it derives its roots.

Previously within the Tithing of Parkstone, which prior to 1833 was itself part of the large parish of Kinson and Great Canford, Lilliput did not become a parish in its own right until the 1960s. The Chapel of the Holy Angels in Lilliput Road was built in 1874 as a chapel-of-ease to St Peter's in Ashley Cross; although negotiations took place with the Ecclesiastical Commissioners in the early 1900s, it was not until 1962 that The Reverend Sargent became the first Vicar of the parish, as opposed to Priest-in-Charge.

Looking further back into the past, we learn from C. Cochrane' s book 'Poole Bay and the Purbeck' of the industry which existed in the area. A saltpan is mentioned on the Canford Manor Shore as early as 1142 and Lord Mountjoy established the alum and copperas mines in the mid-1500s, whilst saltings or salterns were later constructed and possibly remained until the 1820s. We know that in the latter part of the 1800s and early 1900s there was extensive agriculture, particularly on the landward side of Sandbanks Road. Lilliput began to be developed in the 1930s and is now an elegant residential area with every available space being used for new dwellings.

The origins of the name are unclear. 'The Place Names of Dorset' by A.D. Mills mentions Lillypute 1783 and Lilliput 1811 0 S, and I am indebted to Ken Pizey for showing me a 1785 Admiralty Chart 'Survey of the South Coast' by Lieutenant Murdoch Mackenzie which marks the spot 'Etipute' with a nearby 'summerhouse'. On the Register of Voters for 1885-6 the district is shown as Lilliput.

The two people who have been named as having some connection with the appellation are Jonathan Swift and Isaac Gulliver. Jonathan Swift 1667-1745, later Dean Swift of Saint Patrick's Cathedral in Dublin, was born in that city; he was an Anglo-Irish satirist and has been described as one of the greatest masters of English prose. His masterpiece 'Travels Into Remote Nations of the World' more popularly titled 'Gulliver's Travels' was published anonymously in 1726; it has been suggested that he wrote the book in Poole but this cannot be confirmed and seems unlikely. Three names though still serve to remind us of his book - Gulliver Close, Dean Swift Crescent and Lagado Close.

A famous wealthy smuggler who was granted a pardon (probably in 1782) and progressed to a second career as a banker, may also have some connection with the name of Lilliput. Isaac Gulliver was born in Wiltshire in 1745 (the year of Jonathan Swift's death) and died in 1822, being buried in Wimborne Minster. He had associations with a number of Dorset villages - Kinson, West Moors, Corfe Mullen, Long Crichel, Sixpenny Handley and lived at Flag Farm (once called Lilliput Farm), adjacent to the Luscombe Valley, for a few years. There is a suggestion that there might just have been a tunnel linking the property with Brownsea Island, which would have been very handy for his smuggling. Heathland then covered most of the surrounding area and this, too, would have been useful for moving the contraband. The Luscombe Valley is now a Nature Reserve.

Many words of praise have been written about the open space known as Evening Hill. A 1932 Poole Guide 'Gateway to Dorset' describes it thus:-

'The view from Lilliput Hill on the Sandbanks Road is enjoyed by some even more than that from Constitution Hill. Here one may appreciate at closer range the beauty of haven waters and open sea, inlet and headland, sand dunes and white cliffe, hills and heathland, while the crafts of every description, on business or pleasure bent, add interest and animation to the scene. It is because of the glorious sunsets that may be seen from its summit in the peaceful calm of eventide, that Lilliput Hill has been appropriately renamed Evening Hill - sunsets which gladdened the heart of Turner, and were the inspiration of some of his best pictures. There is a splendid mile long promenade from East Dorset Sailing Club Headquarters to the pleasure grounds at Sandbanks, and in the Lilliput district are some charming rural walks, with exquisite vistas of the Dorset Lakeland'.

The late Harry Ashley (Leo), Yachting Correspondent for the then Bournemouth Evening Echo for many years, came to Poole in 1936 from Weymouth, watched the sunset from Evening Hill and fell in love with the harbour.

It is thanks to The Mayor, Aldermen and Burgesses of the Borough of Poole that local people and visitors alike are able to enjoy the freedom of access to Evening Hill. On 30th

December 1912, Poole Corporation bought three plots of land, 'situated on the Flag Farm Estate at Parkstone', from The Right Honourable Humphrey Napier Baron Alington for £725.00. No buildings were ever to be erected and the Corporation were to maintain the space for Public Walks and Pleasure Grounds; no trees or timber were to be allowed to grow to such a height as to interfere with the sea views from the adjoining property (Witley). It seems that the Corporation would be allowed to erect shelters or a bandstand but the site of these would have to be approved by the vendor.

Other names on the Conveyance include The Right Honourable Frederic Baron Wolverton and The Honourable Charles William Augustus Montagu. Also mentioned was Mr Francis John Bramston Beckford, who lived at Witley on the corner with Crichel Mount Road (see the chapter on East Dorset Sailing Club). Dates in 1888,1902 and 1911 are referred to in connection with several other names on the Conveyance.

On the top of Evening Hill is a stone plinth marking the association of Lord Baden-Powell and Scouting with Poole; it was unveiled by Lady Olave Baden-Powell GBE on 11th March 1967.

Poole Borough Council is responsible for the maintenance of Evening Hill and the Management Plan 1996-2006, put together by the Countryside Section of the Open Spaces Services, is available from the Civic Centre.

CHAPTER ONE
CHAPEL OF THE HOLY ANGELS

Before 1891 Reverend Charles Druitt, Reverend C W Sillifant and Reverend J W Gregory served the Chapel of the Holy Angels from Parkstone St Peter's.

1892-1912	Reverend C M Gane
1912-1915	Reverend Henry T H Rountree
1915-1927	Reverend R St Lo Auber
1927-1937	Reverend D A G Muir
1937-1940	Reverend Martin William Willson MA
1941-1944	Reverend Green
1944-1952	Reverend Thomas Patrick Hamerton
1952-1978	Reverend Marshall Sargent MA. First as Priest-in-Charge, then as Vicar of the Parish, independent from St Peter's.
1978-1989	Reverend Basil Watkins-Jones
1989-	Reverend Colin Hodge (Vicar Colin)

The Reverend Charles Druitt and Parishioners,
including the Cornibeer family, 1880.

'A horrid Chapel in buff brick' is Pevsner's description of the Chapel of the Holy Angels in Lilliput Road, and Kelly's Directory of 1923 described it as 'a small edifice of white brick'. It may not have any external architectural merit but step inside and you will find a pleasing and bright interior with many interesting features; with seating for 200 people.

Noted in a 'Parkstone Reminder' as being 'near Salterns', the Chapel of the Holy Angels was opened under the Bishop's Licence on 3rd October 1874, to serve the Canford Cliffs, Sandbanks and Salterns portions of the Parish of St Peter's, Ashley Cross.

A chapel-of-ease to St Peter's, it was built by public subscription on a small piece of land given by Captain F J Butts, who then lived at Salterns House, off Brownsea View Avenue. A plaque inside the Chapel reads as follows:-

'To the Glory of God and in memory of the late Captain Frederick John Butts 77th Regiment who served with great distinction throughout the Crimean War and carried the colours of his Regiment at the battle of Alma. These, with his portrait, are now in St Paul's Cathedral. He gave the site of this church in 1874, the chancel screen was built by him in 1891, and in 1906 the new screen, choir stalls and other embellishments were given to her husband's memory by Mary Butts. This stone further records the fact that the Vicar of the Parish (Canon Dugmore) undertakes for himself and as far as he lawfully may for his successors in the incumbency that the chancel of the Church of the Holy Angels shall not be pulled down or structurally altered by them or under their directions except with the permission previously obtained from the administrators or assigns of the said Captain F J Butts'.

I am indebted to Mrs Dorothy M Parish for lending me the Centenary booklet put together by Reverend Marshall Sargent, who was Vicar at the time of the Centenary in 1974. He commented that the original chapel must have been a quaint building. 'It consisted of no more than the centre nave, the red tile floor being that over which the feet of one hundred years of worshippers have trod. The chapel was heated by an outside furnace, the flue of which ran under the floor across the west end. The top of the flue was of sheet metal which got hot and radiated warm air through a grating. The font drained on to the flue, so at Baptisms there must have been steam as well as heat.'

A postcard
The Reverend C M Gane 1892-1912

As a memorial to the Mission of 1881 the north aisle was built by public subscription; Captain Butts erected the chancel and oak screen in 1891, and 1898 saw the addition of the south aisle. A highly decorated Screen, reproduction of a 15th C design, was presented in 1906 by Captain Butts widow (who had become Mrs Colville Hyde on her second marriage) together with the choir stalls and a stencilled organ case, both designed by Bodley. Around this time the pulpit from St Peter's was installed, and possibly the font and lectern also came from there.

The Centenary booklet comments on the surprisingly large numbers attending services in so sparsely populated an area - 65 were present at the 3.30 pm Evensong on the Sunday after Ascension; whilst on Whit Sunday 1880, at which the Bishop for Madagascar (R Kestell Cornish) preached there were 79, and on the sixth anniversary, combined with Harvest Festival, there were 122 present at Evensong. However, there was no service on Friday 21st January 1881 due to the Great Snow Storm which began on the previous Monday night.

In March 1881, the burial is recorded of James Cornibeer custodian of the Chapel of the Holy Angels; he was a coastguard and lived in Chapel Terrace on the other side of the road. Sunday 3rd April that year was the 'Day of the Heath Fire' when it was reported that all the sidesmen from St Peter's came to strip the Chapel of its furniture because of the fear of everything going up in flames. As the heath fire is not mentioned again, we have to assume that disaster was averted.

On a happier note the Chapel Flag (Blue Ensign) was hoisted for the first time on 15th August 1886 by Mrs Damer; the flagpole apparently stood where the War Memorial is now. The Dawson Damers lived at The Elms, which was the venue for garden parties and Sunday School treats.

22 members of the Choir c1960

The first resident priest-in-charge was The Reverend C M Gane 1892-1912; he lived at Heatherlands in Bingham Avenue and stayed for 20 years. During the early 1900s negotiations with the Ecclesiastical Commissioners were made with a view to Lilliput becoming a separate parish with Mr Gane as Vicar. The scheme had the blessing of all concerned, but fell through on account of the north extension being roofed with corrugated iron, and the Commissioners did not think it worthy of a parish church. The numbers attending the Chapel of the Holy Angels had continued to increase, although they declined for a short while when the Church of the Transfiguration in Chaddesley Glen came into being in 1912.

Predecessor to the present church hall was the church room with a corrugated iron roof built in 1903; it was the scene of social activities for 60 years and part of the time was an Infants School led by Miss Maud Light. Before 1914 a Miss Bussey, who lived on Evening Hill, used to produce plays with the village children in the church room.

During the ministry of The Reverend R St Lo Auber 1915-1927 the windows were filled with stained glass, the west window being particularly beautiful; these were given by Stanley Hilson Burgess and dedicated on 10th March 1918 by the Vicar of St Peter's, Reverend R E Adderley.

The incumbent for the ten years 1927-1937 was The Reverend D A G Muir. He was the first priest-in-charge to occupy Gowrie, renamed The Parsonage, three doors from Heatherlands in Bingham Avenue; this was the gift of Major Garton, who it is believed lived in Lilliput House. Reverend Muir had the reputation of being the finest preacher in Parkstone and had preached in every church in the Deanery, save one. The Vicar of that particular church (who was not named) was apparently adamant in his refusal!

The outbreak of the Second World War in September 1939 interrupted The Reverend Martin Willson's ministry 1937-1940. He went away as a Chaplain to the Forces and after the war joined the Religious Broadcasting Unit at the BBC.

When The Reverend Green 1941-1944, who had been a missionary in Ceylon, became priest-in-charge The Parsonage was still occupied by Martin Willson's family, and initially Reverend Green had to make do with sleeping in the church room! During the war years it had also been used as a canteen for troops stationed in the area and a Mrs Charles was awarded the OBE for her work in this connection.

Before the arrival of The Reverend Marshall Sargent in 1952, the incumbent for eight years had been The Reverend T P Hamerton 1944-1952, who left to become Vicar of three country parishes in Northamptonshire. The Reverend Sargent's ministry covered the years 1952-1978 and in the first ten years he was priest-in-charge, but in 1962 became the first Vicar of the parish. He wrote in the Centenary booklet: 'The church was consecrated on 31st July by Bishop Anderson after unbelievably protracted negotiations with the Commissioners!

A Sunday School group - John and Jean Barnes
at left of back row c 1980
Courtesy: Jean Barnes

Induction of Reverend Colin Hodge
The choir, visiting and local Clergy
September 1989
Courtesy: Jean Barnes

It was right of course that Lilliput should become a parish, for she had always had her own independent life from the Mother Church. At the same time, the great debt owed to St Peter's is gratefully acknowledged'.

The fine reredos, designed by G Baden Beadle and made by Faith Craft, was erected in 1955 and a few alterations carried out including the disposal of the old rush-bottom chairs, 'the creaking of which could be heard on Brownsea Island'. Oak pews, designed and made by Kingsbury and Son, replaced these chairs and the church was re-roofed and an oil-fired boiler installed.

A notable event in 1963 was the dedication of the new church hall by the Bishop of Sherborne on Michaelmas Day. This had been built on the jungle to the east of the church (next to Links Garage) and enabled the old church room to be demolished and the present Vicarage erected on that site. Finance for these properties came from the Commissioners, interest free loans from the Diocese and contributions from parishioners.

The church was enlarged in 1966 by an extension of the main sanctuary and the addition of a Lady Chapel on the north side of the chancel. The Centenary booklet comments 'it made an already beautiful church into something approaching a gem', and made particular reference to the Statue of Our Lady and Child designed by Francis Stephens ARCA. On a practical note and a great improvement, the old candle chandeliers were converted to electricity.

Other interesting and attractive features include an engraved glass south door and the Triptych Sculpture. The glass door has nine separate designs with a central Trinity symbol, and reminds me of the magnificent windows in Moreton Church. In a wooden frame, the Triptych has a white marble pietà in the central panel, gleaming silver angels in each side panel and gold cherubs across the top. Pevsner described it thus: 'The mixture of materials is restless, the execution in each of them graceful and delicate'.

The history of any church is not complete without information regarding the parishioners who supply the spiritual and social aspect of a parish. An anecdote in the Centenary booklet makes interesting reading. One bitter winter's morning The Reverend Sargent chanced to look out of the vestry window as the 7.40 am bus crept up the hill. The road was like glass and on the opposite side stood Grace and Dorothy Clough with another lady; hesitantly they tried the road with one foot and then drew back. A consultation followed and, to his astonishment, he saw them cross the road on their hands and knees. They explained later that they were not going to be done out of going to church, and in any case they had to cross the road to get the bus back home!

Other names mentioned are Miss Corbould and Miss Osborn, Mrs Speer, Olive Godden and Miss Parkes who were handy with their needles and made vestments, altar linen, albs and surplices for the church, and Mrs Margaret Rogers who brought up six sons at number one Chrysanthemum Cottages opposite the church. A young lad, Ernest Baker, used to model for Mrs Butts, who painted him dressed in a felt hat and smock, for which he received one shilling (5p). One day Mrs Butts asked him what he did with it, expecting that he spent it on sweets. His answer, 'oh no Ma'am, I give it to my mother to buy bread with', had the immediate effect of increasing his modelling fee to half-a-crown (2s.6d. or 12½p).

The Reverend Basil Watkins-Jones and his wife Pamela with Mr Ivor Snook - 1989
Courtesy: Jean Barnes

Names associated with the Sunday School include Miss Evans, Miss M Ffrench, Miss K Crokat, Bessie Snell, Miss Biles, Mrs Cherry, Mrs Jean Barnes (1956-1995), Mrs Phyllis Galton and in recent years Miss Grace Williams. Retired priests have happily acted as assistant priests over the years and plaques can be seen in the church to Father Claude Hinscliff 1874-1964, a former Queen's Chaplain Canon Ralph Creed Meredith 1887-1970, and Raymond Wilkinson Lay Reader.

Honorary Assistant Priest from 1980-1986 was The Reverend John D Barnes; he and his wife Jean have been closely involved with the Chapel of the Holy Angels since 1953, running the youth club in the 1960s with Mr and Mrs Golton, supervising the Sunday School and each taking their turn as sidesmen and church wardens.

John Barnes was a late ordinand, being ordained in 1969 after serving as a pilot in the RAF and as a Senior Captain with British Airways. In his early days he had the privilege of introducing King George VI in one of the Royal Christmas Broadcasts on the radio. The previous hour had been a round-up of interviews with interesting people from around the world and John Barnes, piloting a BOAC plane over Orly, France was the last one to speak before King George himself. Since her husband's untimely death in 1986, Jean Barnes has continued to serve the church in many ways being a member of the Parish Church Council and in the choir, was Church Warden with Mr Ivor Snook 1987-1990 and 1991-1993 with Mr Derek Moore. Formerly the Enrolling Member for the Mothers' Union and Deanery Chairman, Jean is now Archdeanery Chairman for Dorset, and is also Chairman of the Governors for Lilliput First School.

The Reverend Colin Hodge (Vicar Colin)

Church of the Holy Angels in Lilliput Road
1998

Organisations connected with the Chapel of the Holy Angels include the Mothers' Union and the Mother/Toddler Group; the 1st Lilliput Brownies celebrated their 20th anniversary at the end of 1998 with Sharon Keen as the current Brownie Guider. Unfortunately the Guide Company which began in 1981 was disbanded in 1995. The Angel Players are a strong drama group with around 30 members; starting in 1983 with a Nativity play, two major productions are now staged each year.

The church hall plays an important role in the local community, being used for outside activities such as Antique Fairs, W I Meetings, Adult Education Classes and as a Polling Station.

The Chapel of the Holy Angels has one interesting distinction and is unusual in that it is the only church within its parish, there being no others of any other denomination.

CHAPTER TWO

LILLIPUT FIRST SCHOOL

Lilliput CE (VC) First School in Lilliput Road was officially opened in December 1974 by the then Mayor of Poole, the late John Norman. The new pupils had, however, arrived at the start of the autumn term in September and this had given the staff a little time to overcome some of the problems associated with a completely new school.

Both coming from Courthill School in Parkstone, Miss Barbara Graves was the first Headteacher and her deputy Mrs June Lush. Other staff included Mrs Jenny Jones, Mrs Noonan, Ms Marilyn Davies, Miss Floyd and Welfare Assistant Mrs Cherry Cotterell.

Prior to the 1970s children were able to begin their primary education either at St Peter's, close to the church in Ashley Cross (now commercial premises) or Courthill (still in existence) until they reached eleven years of age, and then moved on to secondary schools. Now the 4-8 year old children attend a First School and go on to the Middle School, which is Baden-Powell and St Peter's, until the age of thirteen before continuing their education at senior level. Baden-Powell and St Peter's Middle School opened in 1988 and is in Mill Lane, Parkstone.

The Lilliput First School opened with 120 children in the 6-7 age group, some of whom had come from St Peter's, and Miss Graves remembers that the first term was rather difficult in that much of the furniture and equipment had not actually arrived and staff and children made do with far from perfect conditions. 'Adaptability was a lesson in itself'.

In the early days school meals were prepared on the premises and dinner ladies would be on duty to look after the children during meal times, thus giving the teachers an hour to themselves. The post of dinner lady was welcome part-time work for mothers with young families since the hours and school holidays coincided.

One such lady from Lilliput Road described it as a delightful school, with the exceptional green playground surrounded by fir trees. She recalls the annual summer fêtes, jumble sales and the Nativity plays. With strong connections to the Church of the Holy Angels next door, regular visits would take place; the children would tip-toe into church in a suitably hushed fashion and their parents would join them for the end of term service. This contact still continues and Mrs Jean Barnes, Chair of the Governors, frequently takes groups of children into the church where they enjoy brass rubbing and copying the patterns from the kneelers and stained glass windows.

Initially pupils came from the immediate catchment area with many of them walking through 'the lanes' from Whitecliff and the Conifer Park Estate, but that has changed and some children now come from further afield; 'cars jam the road twice a day'.

Many past pupils will remember the late Mr Leslie Hayward. For some years he was the caretaker and the 'lollipop man', and even after retirement continued as a playground helper each morning. A hairdresser by trade (in Lilliput Square), it is believed that Les Hayward's war record (WWII) included distinguished service on the North Sea convoys. For many years he helped run the Lilliput Sea Scouts, initially in the old Mission Hall opposite the Chapel of the Holy Angels (now a private residence) and later at their headquarters in Turks Lane.

He was a most conscientious caretaker at the school and kept the premises spotless, but he also had a true interest in the children and would always talk to the new pupils and help them overcome any problems.

Several branches of the Hayward family lived locally, and there is a story of Les Hayward's uncle Arthur, who after watching the television coverage of the First Moon Landing, declared that it was all a hoax and that the filming had been done over at Studland!

*The Reverend Colin Hodge with children
at Lilliput First School 1990*

The school uniform is grey trousers with red tee shirts for the boys and red or tartan skirt with grey tunics for the girls. The present Headteacher is Mrs Liz Long and her staff include Mrs J Jones, Mrs C Chambers, Miss M Potter, Mrs J Adkins, Miss C Parsons, Miss H Davison, Mrs S Burriss, Mrs C Harvey and Welfare Assistant Mrs C Cotterell. Both Mrs Jenny Jones and Mrs Cherry Cotterell joined the staff when the school opened in 1974. The number of pupils has increased over the years and there are now 240, thus necessitating extensions and further improvements. In March 1993 a new reception block was opened by the Mayor of Poole, the late H C R Ballam OBE and the Bishop of Sherborne, Right Reverend John Kirkham - who also opened and blessed the new library in 1999.

The three schools, Courthill First School, Baden-Powell and St Peter's Middle School and Lilliput First School are planning ahead for the year 2000 with a complete school photograph, a summer Millennium Ball and a Commemorative Plate.

We know there was a church school in Lilliput Road in the early 1900s which existed for a number of years, and when the present name of Lilliput First School emerged an elderly resident was heard to comment that it was NOT the first school there and that someone had got their facts wrong! A letter about this first school published in the Poole Advertiser in 1979 makes interesting reading. Mrs Margaret Fellows (née Tucker) was born in one of the Fellside Cottages in Bingham Avenue in 1910 and attended the school in her early years. One day a lady called at the school to choose someone to blow the church organ for her to practise during the dinner hour.

Margaret was chosen and on most weekdays she was in the church vestry pulling the organ handle while Miss Slade practised; as it was during the years of WWI it is probable that the usual organist was away on war service. Margaret was paid three old pennies (1p) but if she was not required for the full hour, this was reduced to two pennies plus an apple.

We learn from Margaret's letter that the school was then maintained by the local gentry, Miss Light was the headmistress and a young woman from the village taught the juniors. Margaret indicated that the children received a fine education with much emphasis on good manners and religion; they acted in plays with proceeds going to the Soldiers and Sailors fund.

Margaret Fellows would have been a pupil at the school during the First World War (1914-1918) and her diary tells us that the children would gather acorns for the war effort from the many oak trees thriving in the area. The acorns were used as filling for shells, and it is possible that those collected by the school children might have gone to the Holton Heath Munition Factory at Sandford, near Wareham.

CHAPTER THREE

LILLIPUT SQUARE

In 1930 Lilliput Square was described as east and west - there were only four shops - Bertram H Bishop newsagent, S G S Harris dairy, Perrett and Batt grocers (with a branch at Ashley Cross) and Dorset Lake Garage motor engineers. The development of the parade of shops and Salterns Court , as they are today, took place at the end of the 1930s. What is now Salterns Hotel was built in 1934 or 1935 and the first trader to open his doors in Lilliput Square was John's the butchers in 1939, just in time for the start of WWII on 3rd September.

It is interesting to find that many of the shops are still trading in the same line of business as when they opened in 1939. At some point the numbers seem to have changed slightly, which has been confusing and, of course, some properties have been divided and others expanded into next door.

Mrs S Rowntree Dental Surgeon is at 296 Sandbanks Road. In 1939 it was 'The Lilliput Wine Stores' (there is a possibility that this was run by Fred Karno, the legendary music hall artiste), 1961 Findlater, Mackie, Todd wine and spirit merchants, and in 1975 Cameo budget boutique. Jane Naden International Hair Stylists should feel at home since it has always been a ladies hairdresser; in 1939 it was Miss C Grace, 1961 A and N Waite and 1975 'Therese'.

Recently changing its name to Harriet's, the restaurant at 292 has had various names and owners in the last few years; Barrie the Fish, well-known in the area having a wet fish shop in Westbourne and briefly one in Canford Cliffs, refurbished 292 and changed the external appearance. Next it became Chez Maman, Chandlers and then a bistro Cafe Bar Provence. It started life in 1939 with a Miss C E Somervell as a gown shop, became a restaurant in 1961 'The Lilliput Inn' and in 1975 fresh owners called it 'The Lilliput Coffee House'. The shop next door on the corner at 290, now May's estate agents, was Lilliput Ironmongery and Marine Company in 1939, then Arthur Bray yacht brokers in 1961 and Bolloms dry cleaners in 1975.

Sandbanks Road, Lilliput Square looking west
c 1947. Note BOAC sign on right
Courtesy: Poole Museums Service

Crossing Dorset Lake Avenue we come to 6 Salterns Court which has always been a chemist. Now called the Lilliput Pharmacy, it was opened in 1939 by Percy Osmond MPS FSMC and he was still there in 1961, followed by D J Shakesheff in 1975. 5 Salterns Court is now familiar as Siesta selling smart casual wear; Harold Taylor was there in 1939 as a radio engineer, Southern Radio and Television in 1961, and 1975 Siesta was described simply as 'outfitters'. 284 Sandbanks Road (4 Salterns Court) is Poole Harbour Board Sailing but will be remembered by many folk as Matley's newsagents, first of all in 1939 it was Harold N Matley, then 1961 and 1975 A Matley and Son. 3A Salterns Court is Norris and Owen estate agents. In 1939 Gerald Hopkins traded there as a building contractor 'decorators and repairers to all classes of property', 1961 it was Fox and Sons auctioneers and estate agents (also Shoecraft boot repairs) and in 1975 Richard Owen ARICS chartered surveyor, estate agent and valuer. Barclays Bank is on the corner of Salterns Way with Perrins Stevenson solicitors next door. A boot repairer, Ernest S Jones, shared the premises in 1939 with fruiterer George Alcock, whilst 1961 saw Mr Mears as the fruiterer, and Martins Bank there with Mr T Hunter as manager, and in 1975 it became Barclays Bank.

Crossing Salterns Way the first premises we come to contains Financial Advisers Francis Rhys and Partners at 266 Sandbanks Road. In 1939 K V Cowie was there as manager of Lloyds Bank; as well as John Jagger builders, and as Lloyds Bank still in 1961 and 1975 with Mr A E Horton as manager. Next door is now Lloyds estate agents. It opened in 1939 as Burden and Sons grocers, carried on in the same trade in 1961 and 1975 with J and D Harding, and C D Cooper. 262 was Lilliput Stores newsagents and Post Office. In March 1999 a change of ownership brought it into the hands of the Dillons Group. It was a gentleman's hairdressers in 1939 with Robert J Spurin and Leslie Hayward took over in 1961; there was also a tobacconist Hedley G Childs who was followed by A G Payne in 1975. 260 is also part of Lilliput Stores (Dillons) and was originally a confectioners run by Edgar Aspin, then W F Vousden described himself as a baker in 1961, and 1975 it will be remembered as a very popular Home Made Cake Shop and Bakers.

Gullivers the butchers (previously John's) is next door at 258. Mrs Mary Burden, whose family have always been there, told me that they were the first shop to open in the new parade, and were Martins Bank fourth client. Some customers then, despite the war, were quite demanding and one lady from Sandbanks was most particular about her meat - she chose the joints herself and wanted them hung but insisted that her meat should not make contact with any other, neither should it be touched by anyone else! Families owning houses in Sandbanks then included Peck's Potted Meats and Owbridge's Lung Tonic. Mary Burden was fascinated by the flying boats on the harbour and would watch the activity whenever possible - one day she heard what she thought was a craft coming in very low, only to find it was a German bomber which dropped one of its load into Poole Park lake. The shop is now run by Mrs Burden's son Michael Johns together with Peter Young. The Victoria Wine off-licence is at 256; it seems likely that Walter Knight, draper (later called Knight's of Parkstone with a shop at Ashley Cross) had both 256 and 254 Sandbanks Road. In 1975 one part was used by Lilliput Hardware and around 1996 became Lillipets, which is now closed.

Salterns Court, Lilliput Square 1998

Lilliput Square in the snow 19.2.78.
The lone figure is Mr Harry Robinson.

Sometime after 1975 Dr Frederick Rutland's surgery (later joined by Dr Goodrich and Dr Walder) was above number 254, it later moved to 1 Salterns Way and eventually developed into an extensive practice, Lilliput Surgery, at Lindisfarne, 1 Elms Avenue with Drs B H Goodrich, G P Walder, J D Buckmaster, Susan M Thomas and Andrew F K Rutland. The Practice Manager, Miss Heather Liversedge, has been with them since 1982. This medical practice had its origins on the opposite side of Sandbanks Road in Lilliput Square with the surgery of physician and surgeon Edgar R Bowes at 277, and in 1961 of Brian W Rhodes and R C Howard Tripp. Three doctors - Tripp, Walker and Rutland were there in 1975, and it is now a residential home, Lilliput House, run by Mr and Mrs R A Bettison.

Still on the north east side of the road coming from Poole, there was a school more or less where the well-illuminated Texaco petrol station now stands, and it has been suggested that there may have once been a tithe barn thereabouts. The 1939 Kelly's states that between Blakedene Road and Brownsea View Avenue, Reginald E S Birdsall was proprietor of the Parkway Garage, in 1961 under the same name it was described as a service station and in 1975 the name had become Lillyput Service Station. Between Brownsea View Avenue and the surgery in 1939 was St Petroc and Holly Cottage; apparently taking up three plots was The Green Glade Café and Tea Gardens under the ownership of Mr and Mrs P M Cocke. This had disappeared by 1961 and Brownsea Court has taken its place.

The Oddbins site, on the corner with Anthonys Avenue, was not developed in 1939 but by 1961 there was a grocers L and M Rushton and by 1975 this had been taken over by Gough Brothers wine and spirit merchants. The Clock, a small development of flats built in the mid-1990s, completes our tour of Lilliput Square. In 1939 it was Dorset Lake Garage (Albert E Fancy and Albert Cole props) and in 1961 Parkway Garage showrooms and Parkway Marine, marine stores/dealers, and in 1975 still the same name but described as boat distributors. The company now trades from a building at the Blue Lagoon next to the Lilliput Sailing Club.

Lilliput Square 1998

CHAPTER FOUR

LILLIPUT ROAD

The 1918 Kelly's Directory tells us that, what is now known as Lilliput Road, was then called Salterns Hill and was also known as Lilliput Hill; but this is not to be confused with Evening Hill which was once Lilliput Hill Road and even further back Cload's Hill.

Thirty properties are listed for Lilliput Road in 1918 including George Rogers grocer and post office, Chapel of the Holy Angels and Lilliput Mission Hall which became the headquarters of the 1st Lilliput Sea Scouts and is now a private residence. These properties reached as far as Bingham/Compton Avenue.

In 1939 there were eight properties on the north side of Lilliput Road up to the Chapel of the Holy Angels, then Gale's Garage and another twelve up to Compton Avenue. Mr Arthur R Noonan (brother-in-law of George Rogers at the post office across the road) lived at Silverdale (number 19) on the corner with Dean Swift Crescent, and he was apparently in charge of the Lilliput Working Men's Club situated three houses further up the road. By 1961 a few more properties had been built and the Working Men's Club described as a day nursery (Growing Time Nursery), whilst by 1975 Hurst Hill had appeared, together with Harbour Prospect as well as the new Lilliput First School and the Holy Angels Vicarage.

There was only one property on the south side between the garage (now The Clock) and Gulliver Close in 1939 - this was Peatbank (number six) owned by Major William Ernest Grice Ord-Statter. Then came Rose Cottages and Pine View up the lane, George Rogers and Son motor garage and post office, Plumtree Cottages, Chapel Terrace, Pine and Oak Villas, Boy Scouts (1st Lilliput Group) headquarters F W Claridge group scoutmaster, Chrysanthemum Cottages, W B Chinchen builder (where is now Lagado Close), Vale View Cottages and Alington Cottages. A letter from Mrs Margaret Fellows published in a 1979 'Poole Advertiser' mentioned that at one stage there was a pump at the top of the hill from which some of the cottagers fetched their water; and next door was Jenny Bascombe's bakery - she baked her bread and delivered it in her donkey cart. The property on the golf course side of Bingham Avenue was, in 1961, a police house for the Dorset County Constabulary.

Believed to have been purpose built as a shop in 1897, 22 Lilliput Road was described in 1939 as a grocer and post office H G Rogers, 1961 it was G Rogers and Son motor garage and post office; in 1975 L R W Dale grocer. An unused invoice from the 1930s is headed Post Office, Lilliput G Rogers and Son, Est 1897, Telephone Number 22 Canford Cliffs - Coal, Coke, Firewood and Grocery Stores - Lilliput Garage - Cars for Hire; an old photograph shows a

The old Post Office in Lilliput Road in George Rogers time -
note the missing 'L' in Post Office sign. c early 1900s.
Courtesy: Mrs Dolly Dale

pony and trap outside the shop with the coal and coke stores on the right and a misspelled 'Liliput' Post Office sign. It seems that the trap was kept in the coal store and the pony was stabled in a barn at the top end of the lane. The exterior of the building has changed very little over the years and is still a distinctive feature on Lilliput Road, retaining as it does the Edward VIII post box and the original design telephone call box.

Until his death in 1991 and her retirement in 1997 Leslie Dale and his wife Dorothy (Dolly) were well known to the local people and Mrs Dale told me what had brought them to Lilliput in 1965. They had run a filling station in Weston-Super-Mare and began to think of retiring to the south coast. Coming to the area to look round, it was pure chance that brought them past number 22, and liking the look of the shop, with its old long armed Shell petrol pump and iron steps, Mr Dale popped inside to have a chat whilst Mrs Dale took the opportunity of inspecting the nearly completed bungalows opposite. It appears that their timing was good for George Rogers was on the point of retiring! After taking over the business, they were disappointed to find that Mr Rogers had not kept up the licence needed for the petrol pump, and that same year the Post Office was moved down to Lilliput Square. Mr and Mrs Rogers lived in Dean Swift Crescent in their retirement; and other family members close by were Mrs Noonan on the corner and Mrs Janes near the Scout headquarters further up Lilliput Road.

It is through the efforts of Mr and Mrs Dale that the telephone box, which was erected in 1954 and is in the style of the original 1936 design by Giles Gilbert Scott, still stands. In the mid-1980s British Telecom wanted to replace it with a modern one, but after fighting to keep what has become part of our familiar heritage, Mr and Mrs Dale won the battle in 1987.

Many local people relied on Mr Dale's taxi service over the years and he also gave his time as a volunteer for the Hospital Car Service, taking blind people to day centres. He is remembered for his cheerfulness and kindness to everyone, whether it was delivering groceries to the housebound or helping anyone in need; and on one occasion lending money to his passenger for the railway fare since they had left home without their wallet.

Although over 80 years of age when she closed the shop and retired in April 1997, Mrs Dale had been determined to let the shop reach its centenary! Still within the family, the premises are now used by Michael Gregory and Lee Scott for Selva Marine, a parts distribution company.

THE WATERWORKS

In Lawrence Popplewell's book 'High Horse Manger' published in 1987, he quoted a paragraph from the Bournemouth Times of 27th June 1923 which mentioned the disappearance of a conspicuous landmark. This was the chimney shaft of the old water works at Lilliput, and the task of felling the stack had been a delicate operation owing to the proximity of two dwellings. These properties are described as the Waterworks Cottages in the 1930 Kelly's, occupied by Sidney James Baker and Charles Major, groundstaff for Parkstone Golf Club. The waterworks were situated further along Lilliput Road towards Canford Cliffs where the road runs through the golf course.

Just before 1910 Lord Wimborne, with the intention of creating a golf course, bought 23 acres of land from the Poole Water Company, who had moved their operation out to Corfe Mullen. The sale covered the two original reservoirs, which had been dug out by hand and the sand transported by horse and cart to the other side of Compton Avenue. These freshwater lakes now attract all sorts of wildlife, but despite treatment to reduce the level of naturally occurring alum, attempts to stock them with trout have been disappointing.

The Victorian pumphouse which can be seen from Lilliput Road, was also included in the sale; constructed beneath this building are huge underground reservoirs. In the early 1980s, when Parkstone Golf Club installed a new watering system, these underground reservoirs were drained and opened so that they could be inspected for possible damage. Dick Peach recalled how he viewed with awe the impressive cathedral-like caverns which had been built by the old water company. The two halls were lined with glazed yellow bricks, and except for some minor damage to the roofs caused by tree roots, the structure was in excellent condition and a great tribute to the skills of the Victorian builders. He estimated that the reservoirs could hold about three million gallons of water.

The two cottages alongside the pumphouse were built to house waterworks employees. At one time they were let by the golf club as summer retreats and then eventually rented to two of the groundstaff before remaining empty from 1939 as Sidney Baker and Charles Major left to serve in WWII. It is believed that a number of bombs fell on the golf course and one destroyed the roofs of the two cottages which were unoccupied at the time. The condition of the dwellings gradually deteriorated and they were sold in 1949 to a Mrs Russell-Brown for £1500.00. and in due time were demolished.

Lilliput Road - Victorian Pumphouse - Parkstone Golf Course 1999

Among the groundstaff at Parkstone Golf Club in more recent years was Frank Gillett who was born around 1900 in one of the waterworks cottages. He worked there for 48 years from 1919, and despite receiving lucrative offers from other Clubs maintained his loyalty to Parkstone and remained there until his retirement in 1967. Mr and Mrs Gillett lived at 30 Lilliput Road, which was one of the Plumtree Cottages.

A full and comprehensive History of Parkstone Golf Club was published in 1987 by Mr L C Jenkins, and I am grateful for his courtesy in allowing me to use the above information.

Looking up Lilliput Road 19.2.78.
Centre right is the old Post Office

The names listed for Lilliput Road in the 1918 Kelly's Directory are as follows:-

H Tessier (Salterns Cottage)

George Holder

Frederick Jeans jnr

James Rogers

Harry Hayward

A Hayward

Frank Mabey

George Rogers grocer & Post Office

H Selby

George Curtis

John Oates

Ernest Galton

William Hayward

J Baker

Mrs Old

Thomas Hayward

Mrs Bascombe

Henry Eastwood

Chapel of the Holy Angels

Mrs Marvell

Lilliput Mission Hall

G Gillett

T Rogers

W Galton

Ernest Baker

Allington Cottages:

John Galton

Bert Baker

Mrs Fudge

S Baker

John Pollard

Phone. No. 22 Canford Cliffs.   Established 1897.

Post Office, Lilliput,...........................193

FROM *G. ROGERS & SON,*

Coal, Coke, Firewood & Grocery Stores.

LILLIPUT GARAGE.   —   —   CARS FOR HIRE.

To M...........................

	£	s.	d

Served by...........................

1897 Invoice

The village of Lilliput grew considerably during the 1930s. The parade of shops and Salterns Court, known as Lilliput Square, were constructed on the south west side of Sandbanks Road in the early part of the decade; and Captain Dickie Preston built The Harbour Club on a 'rubbish dump' at the edge of the harbour in 1934 or 1935. On reclaimed land, it was part of the salterns or saltings, and a single track railway ran from there up to George Jennings South Western Pottery which made sanitary stoneware and decorative terracotta products. The railway, believed to have been taken up in 1928, ran along behind The Beehive, probably crossed Sandbanks Road near the Blue Lagoon, over Elgin Road and skirted the cemetery. The rubbish dump is likely to have been the remains of broken pottery mixed with coal being shipped in for the pottery kilns; and the property was built on a concrete raft.

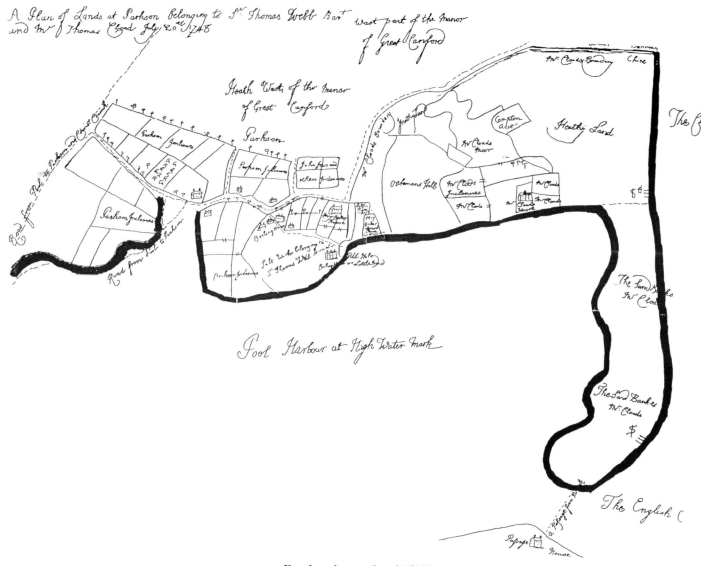

Free hand map dated 1748
Courtesy: Poole Reference Library

Poole Reference Library have a copy of a free hand map dated 20th July 1748 'A Plan of Lands at Parkson belonging to Sir Thomas Webb and Mr Thomas Cload - Part of the Manor of Great Canford'. This shows the area now covered by the Blue Lagoon and Salterns Hotel and Marina as 'Salt Works belonging to Sir Thomas Webb', two 'Boiling Houses' are marked, one very close to the edge of the harbour and the other back towards Sandbanks Road. Close by is a house marked 'Pery Baker'; this might have some connection with The Beehive but the dates of the 1748 map and Peregrine Baker's lease to Frederick Styring 1863, do not tally. A 'Salt Office' is indicated on Isaac Taylor's 1765 map, an O S map of 1811 shows 'salt pans' quite clearly and in 1829 'Salt Office' is still marked. By 1849 a chart of Poole Harbour describes the area as 'Old Salterns' and in 1934 as 'Saltern's Marsh'.

There was, and still is, only one means of vehicular access to The Harbour Club, this being Salterns Way, a turning between the shops in Lilliput Square. Kelly's Directory of 1939 lists 16 houses there, and this had only risen to 19 in 1975; at least one of the original house names is still in use, and a small group of 1930s properties there is part of a National Collection of houses of this particular period and design.

In setting up his combined hotel (Poole Harbour Hotel) and yacht club (The Harbour Club) Richard Frank Preston emphasised the club as the dominant facility, but an event in October 1935 may not have endeared him to the local authorities.

On 28th November that year a lengthy and detailed report appeared in the Poole and Dorset Herald headed 'The Harbour Club Raid - Police Court Hearing Concluded - More Vigilant Control in Future Promised'. This referred to a number of summonses arising out of a police raid on The Harbour Club at Lilliput on 19th October; there were 26 defendants in all. Mr Preston, described as secretary, was charged with not conducting a club, in good faith, and habitually admitting non-members for the purpose of obtaining intoxicating liquor; also charged with supplying intoxicating liquor to 25 persons during non-permitted hours.

The names and addresses of all the defendants, both male and female, were published - many were from Canford Cliffs, Parkstone and Bournemouth with a few from other parts of the country. The magistrates were Mr W Parnell, Councillor A H Johnston, Mr E H May, Mr G Belben, Alderman A Shutler and Alderman A J Dacombe. Prosecuting for the police was Mr A C Templeman; Mr J C Caswell defended Mr Preston and a number of the other defendants. It appears that numerous complaints had been received by the police about the club and they had set up observations over a period of several weeks; evidence was given by Superintendent Swain and Sergeant Brickle regarding the late night drinking activities and the number of vehicles which left the car park in the early hours. Membership of the club was just over 1000 at the time; with 17 letting rooms in the hotel.

A boatyard has been based on the site since the early 1930s, and Cecil Edney began work as a yard hand there at the age of fourteen. There was only a small basin then and just one shipwright under the banner of the Walton Yacht and Launch Company. Later taken over by three men, Messrs Park, Dempster and Scott it was called P D S (Poole) Limited; but the company foundered owing money to, amongst others, Captain Woods Chandlery at the end of Poole High Street. Later owners were South Coast Yachting Services Limited, and marine engineer E Gillam is mentioned in the Kelly's Directories of 1961 and 1975.

Apart from his war service in the Royal Navy, Cecil Edney spent all his working life at the boat yard through all the various owners; he retired in the early 1990s and had seen many changes in the marine industry, in particular with regard to construction techniques and use of materials other than wood. He remembers with pleasure working on a 500 ton coal burning steam yacht; and later when the marina was extended watching the mulberry barges towed in and holes drilled so that they sank in position. His recollections include that of the tennis court, which stood on the site of the present day car park.

The inner dock at Poole Harbour Yacht Club
(now Salterns Marina) c 1950s
Courtesy: Mr John Smith

BOAC Sunderland Flying Boat 'Hawkesbury' G-AGHZ
Courtsey: Wing Commander (Rtd) R W Kemsley

In 1939 the whole site was requisitioned as the Marine Terminal for the Flying Boat Service of British Overseas Airways Corporation (previously Imperial Airways) and was handed back in 1948 when the passenger terminal moved to Hythe, Southampton. During the war years Poole Harbour was Britain's only international airport with twice weekly services to South Africa, India and Australia via Lisbon and East Africa; also, starting in the autumn of 1940, to North America.

Five runways crossed the harbour and passengers would wait in the departure lounge at The Harbour Club, take a short walk along the pier and on to launches which took them out to the flying boats. Statesmen, Ambassadors, high ranking Service personnel, intelligence agents, resistance workers, film stars and entertainers were often among the passengers, and any visiting VIP's received a Guard of Honour from soldiers at Bovington Camp. King George VI and Sir Winston Churchill used the flying boats, as did General de Gaulle. Amongst a group returning from the Quebec Conference in 1943 were Sir Anthony Eden and Lord Louis Mountbatten.

Many passengers travelled incognito as they carried information vital to the progress of the war. A young train spotter of the time remembers being escorted away from the old platform three at Bournemouth West Station when a train with fully blacked out compartments was due. Mr Basil Hodder says that this special train served the flying boat schedules running non-stop, two or three times weekly, usually in late afternoon, from Bournemouth West direct to London's

Victoria Station. Reputed to complete the journey in under two hours, the train was made up of three coaches, a brake van and sometimes a Pullman car which were hauled by a T9 class engine. It was the only direct service to Victoria, not available to other than BOAC passengers and was given a clear road throughout its journey. Among Mr Hodder's other wartime memories is that of bananas, which were so scarce that some children grew up without the pleasure of tasting them. One of the BOAC pilots used to stay at his parents Bournemouth hotel, The Belgravia in Christchurch Road, and sometimes tucked away in the cargo hold on a return journey were bunches of bananas - some of which found their way into our young train spotter's hands!

Passengers booked on an early morning flight from the harbour often stayed overnight at the Harbour Heights Hotel in Haven Road; others used the Sandacres Hotel on Sandbanks where a young apprentice electrician recalls being asked to step to one side as people on 'clandestine missions' came through the door which was guarded by sentries with fixed bayonets. As a lad of 15, Keith Tharme worked for a firm of vetted tradesmen who would be called out to do running repairs at the many hotels in the area being used for Service billets and Government offices. Young though he was and only an apprentice, Keith Tharme was entrusted with major electrical repairs since, as he said 'there was no-one else to do the work, all the older chaps being away in the Services'. He has some interesting memories of those days - 'The Americans were very particular about guarding the front entrance of the hotels being used as accommodation for the Services, but they didn't bother about the ever open back doors past the kitchens, and I often surprised them by finding my way into the building without their knowledge. One hotel I was called to was full of WAAC's and somebody called out a warning 'look out, there's a man around'. They needn't have worried, at the age of 15 I was the one who was embarrassed'!

BOAC Sunderland Flying Boat G-AGJN on Poole Harbour
Courtesy: Wing Commander (Rtd) R W Kemsley

With an armed guard always at the gate, The Harbour Club building was occupied as offices by both the Air Ministry and BOAC, the latter using the right hand side as one faces the entrance. As his first job after leaving school Gordon Cousins was based there as a junior postal clerk with BOAC. A Miss Hardwick was his immediate boss - her father was Marine Superintendent on the Air Ministry side - and a Mr George August, whose secretary was Miss Goldsmith, was in overall charge. 'We were provided with our own dark blue double breasted brass buttoned uniforms and a peaked cap and these were made to measure by H J Travers, outfitters at 124 High Street, Poole. One of my tasks, with a colleague, was to deliver mail to various BOAC departments in the area; a car would call for us early in the morning and off we would go to the Hamworthy depot, offices at 4 High Street, Poole Pottery (also a flying boat reception and departure point), the stevedores offices in Old Orchard, the Blue Lagoon staff restaurant, to Harbour Heights Hotel and out to Hurn'. Gordon's family home had a good view of the harbour and he was able to watch the movements of the flying boats, once witnessing one of them being sprayed with machine gun fire from a German aircraft.

Ron Kemsley served in the Royal Air Force for 40 years starting at Cranwell in 1937 and retiring as a Wing Commander in 1977. As a Flight Lieutenant he arrived in Poole during the winter of 1942, having been seconded by the Air Ministry to BOAC, who themselves were not in a position then to train new flying boat crews. Flight Lieutenant Kemsley had just finished a tour of operations with Bomber Command and was posted as a Radio Officer to Number Two Division which was to fly Sunderlands to the Far East. Previously used on anti-submarine patrols in the Atlantic, the Sunderland flying boats had been converted into luxury air liners and carried 26 passengers - most of whom would have been VIPs. As civilian aircraft 'the freedom of the skies' should have meant that they were not attacked, but this was not always the case.

There was usually a crew of five - the Captain, First Officer, Radio Officer, Flight Engineer and Navigator, and their route to the Far East took them across the Bay of Biscay (France being occupied), Gibraltar, along the North African coast to Cairo, on to Basra and Karachi and so to Calcutta. Following the surrender of the Japanese the route was extended via Rangoon to Singapore and on certain services to Hong Kong. They generally flew during the day and their trip would keep them away for 14/17 days - compensations came in the form of luxury accommodation in such famous hotels as Shepherds and Raffles.

One of Ron Kemsley's particular memories is of an incident which occurred on his birthday, 15th March 1944. The late evening saw considerable enemy air activity along the South Coast which unfortunately coincided with the scheduled service to Calcutta; the first leg being a night flight across the Bay of Biscay to Gibraltar. The prelude was to lay the flare-path in the harbour by the pinnace towing a dozen or so small dinghies, each with a battery powered light, and anchoring in a line at 100 yards or so intervals. After take-off the routine procedure was that twenty minutes into the flight a radio message would be sent confirming 'all well and proceeding'. This was the signal for the coxswain and crew of the pinnace to recover the flare-path.

Some few minutes prior to the appointed time, Murphy's Law came into play. The aircraft developed an engine problem whilst at the same time the flare-path was being hurriedly recovered because of the presence of enemy aircraft. A rapid return to Poole found a mere two flares still in position; and sight of an investigating enemy Night Fighter did much to encourage an immediate landing. The sea was flat calm and mirror-like and this, coupled with the lack of an adequate flare-path resulted in some misjudgement.

Poole Harbour - sailing dinghies amongst the
Flying Boats - after 1945.
Courtesy: S. Sieger

The approach was too steep and consequently the Sunderland went through the surface of the water, coming to rest with one wing submerged; propellers were bent and one wing float torn off. As the aircraft was in danger of turning turtle the crew jettisoned some of the fuel from the submerged wing thus righting the aircraft, although the opposite wing float was partly submerged by the abnormal load.

There was a radio station on the roof of Poole Pottery at Poole Quay, and apparently when the emergency message was received from the crashed aircraft one of the junior operators was in such a hurry to call the appropriate rescue station that he tripped and broke his leg! This resulted in a delay and Ron Kemsley remembers calming the passengers during the wait - one elderly lady asked if it was normal for the water to be half-way up the portholes, and he assured her that it was an everyday occurrence.   None of the passengers panicked, and fortunately obeyed instructions not to smoke - in fact the English stiff upper lip was in evidence, and everyone was taken off safely. As the rescue boat manoeuvred alongside, the Flight Engineer shouted to the coxswain 'to mind the float', and to everyone's surprise a female voice with a Roedean accent answered back 'I know precisely what I'm doing'. Unfortunately, the pinnace did in fact make slight contact with the float. Afterwards Ron commented that, with the exception of the over enthusiastic radio operator, no-one was injured and this was the best birthday present he could have received.

After the war Ron Kemsley continued working with the Sunderlands, being part of the Test Crew for the testing and preparation of aircraft for use on the route, the servicing being carried out at the Hythe Depot near Southampton.   After he married Beryl Cotterill at the Church of the Holy Angels in Lilliput Road on 29th April 1946, they unofficially embarked on a Sunderland flying boat in Poole Harbour which was returning to Hythe, and from there they travelled to Jersey for their honeymoon. They now live in Kent. I have only skimmed the surface of the fascinating history of the flying boats in Poole Harbour, and recommend Leslie Dawson's book 'Wings Over Dorset - Aviation's Story in the South', which contains a long and detailed relevant chapter. A revised edition was published in 1989 by the Dorset Publishing Company in Wincanton, ISBN 0 948699 10 8.

It is thought that after 1948 the name, The Harbour Club, changed to Poole Harbour Yacht Club (PHYC) and around 1950 was for sale at £12,000. It was offered to other yacht clubs in the area but all turned it down. Soon after, however, Mr John Clark, a property entrepreneur from London, acquired the club and boatyard. Described as a pleasant self-made man, he started his working life as a clerk with Wimbledon Council and it is believed that the deal which set him on the road to success was that of buying a bomb site at the Elephant and Castle and, hiring a Rolls Royce and a chauffeur to set the right tone, sold it on to developers.

Already familiar with the area John Clark had bought the house 'Forsyte Shades', above the 15th green of Parkstone Golf Club, for £15,000. in 1945. He was a member of the Club and it appears that Reg Whitcombe, the Professional at Parkstone from 1928 to 1956, had once commented in John Clark's hearing that the house would have made an ideal site for their clubhouse. When 'Forsyte Shades' came on to the market some time later John Clark acquired it and offered to sell to the golf club for the same figure; but his offer was not taken up. After living there for a few years, he sold the house and then bought Poole Harbour Yacht Club in 1948. 'Forsyte Shades' is now a prestigious development of flats.

John Clark had bought PHYC as a speculation and did not spend money on improving the building, and it seems that this was a disappointment to one or two people. For ten years he tried, and failed, to obtain planning permission to demolish it in order to build flats. These would have been no higher than the Club itself and sited on a less obtrusive spot than those which were erected 20 years later. He did, however, improve the boatyard/marina with the major construction of a breakwater - this was made up of old mulberry harbour barges, designed for the D-Day landings in 1944, and which it is believed cost him £10.00 each.

A Parkstone Golf Club occasion at the Branksome Tower Hotel in 1951 John Clark,
owner of PHYC in the 1950s and 1960s is second left with Miss Mary Llewellin, the first
Lady Mayor of Poole, together with Roy Jenkins, Major Latter, Reg Whitcombe and Vernon Haydon.
Courtesy: Mr L C Jenkins

It is said that the Suez Crisis in the mid-1950s gave John Clark an opportunity to use his entrepreneurial skills; knowing that oil tankers capable of the longer journey round South Africa would be required, he purchased a number of rusting tankers, and sold them on at a later date. At the same time he bought himself a 500 ton hospital ship and converted it as his own yacht; with a crew of 18 there were two chefs - one for the crew and one for himself - and it has been suggested that the cost of chartering was £10,000. per month. The name of this yacht was, I believe, 'Mirandus'.

Around 1955 membership of PHYC was down to only 300 and John Clark wanted to close it. But the then Commodore, Mr Greville Humphries, persuaded him to allow the existing members to carry on and to use their own efforts to increase the membership. The subscription was reduced from 12 guineas (£12.60) to four guineas (£4.20) as an inducement, and John Clark permitted them the use of the bar and what was then known as 'the TV alley'. The membership drive was so successful that by the late 1960s there were around 1700 members.

Young people were among the new members and this created a good base for the future years. A water ski section was created which became very popular - John Clark was very supportive of these activities and a ramp was built for their use. Television coverage was organised for one of the Ski Galas and the members produced a huge PHYC banner which gave the Club some publicity. John Clark was instrumental in obtaining a Royal Warrant allowing the Club to fly the defaced Ensign incorporating their own logo.

A PHYC brochure from the early 1960s presented a glowing picture of the harbour suggesting that the 'launch or sailing dinghy enthusiast will find a veritable paradise behind the islands with lovely anchorages at Arne, Shipstal or Russel Quay, and larger vessels can sail as far as 12 miles up the River Frome towards Wareham'. The brochure informed us that the Club provided a modern yachting and social centre with up-to-date facilities for yachtsmen with an attractive social club providing all amenities for social enjoyment and recreation ashore. The Club was to run on the widest possible lines and to cater for all classes of yachtsmen. Sailing and Motor Yacht Sub-Committees would organise events and cruises during the season, and to link up the Club's activities in that direction with other Clubs. The Club would also sponsor and assist the formation of racing groups using 'Class' sailing boats; two groups had already been formed using the Fairey 'Swordfish' and a special Club Class of 18 ft centre plate boats to Camper and Nicholson's design, to be known as the Poole Seagull. It appeared that speed boat racing would NOT be catered for.

The brochure went on to describe the Club building, containing 37 bedrooms with central heating, and 16 bathrooms available for members. The ground floor had a large lounge and dance floor, dining room, snack bar, cocktail bar, men's bar, large bridge room, reading room and a squash court (believed to have been the first in Poole or Bournemouth). A band was in attendance at the week-ends. Facilities for the yacht owner included floating pontoons in the inner harbour adjacent to the car park, a tidal dock, two patent cradles at the slipway, winter storage, workshops and 30 deep water moorings off the pier head.

PHYC was a thriving Club in the 60s and 70s, and members recall that it had a happy, carefree atmosphere with the combination of sailing and social activities working together extremely well. Poole Week in the summer is now run entirely by Parkstone Yacht Club but in those days all the yacht clubs took part and each night of the week a social event was held at a different club.

A programme of events in 1968 covered a wide range of activities including Candlelit Dances, Beatnites, Musical Evenings, a Champagne Party, the Easter Fitting-Out Dinner Dance, August Annual Races - Worbarrow Bay and Poole Bay, Boatowners Dinner, the Annual Laying-Up Ball at the Savoy Hotel in Bournemouth (£3.00 per ticket) and the usual Stag Party Sprat Supper in December. Apparently events were subsidised by 40% from the Members' Social Fund - the Fruit Machines!

Mrs Grace Aldridge, whose husband Ray was Commodore 1973-4, has happy memories of the themed Summer Balls held over a number of years. These were magnificent affairs - everyone dressed in appropriate costumes and there was always a long waiting list for tickets. Particularly remembered is the Viennese Evening, Arabian Nights, Circus Night under the Big Top, a Wild West Evening and the Venetian Ball when a bridge was built across the dock especially for the occasion. The New Year's Event was always a Fancy Dress Ball.

Poole Harbour Yacht Club (now Salterns Marina)
after a storm in the 1950s.
Courtsey: S. Sieger

Mrs Ena Perry was Secretary at PHYC for many many years; a well-liked lady - short of stature but with a lovely personality. Always elegantly dressed Mrs Perry would greet everyone by name, and ask after their children. Although she would have been privy to a lot of social chit-chat, no gossip was ever repeated by her.

The Club may have had one or two extrovert members over the years, but it is probable that Lady Docker is the one remembered by the majority of people. A 1960s socialite, she married the man who made a fortune out of Bentley cars; they owned 'Little Fosters' a house on the cliff top at Chaddesley Glen (now redeveloped) and had a flat near Branksome Chine. Their yacht 'Shimara' was often moored at PHYC and they attended many of the social activities. Lady Docker had an extrovert personality and the national press of the time featured her many extravagant exploits. After one or two unfortunate incidents, Lady Docker was refused entry to the Club.

During the 1980s and early 90s the concept of belonging to a yacht club in order to sail was losing its attraction; yachtsmen did not feel inclined to have the hassle of sitting on committees and the burden of running a club, preferring instead to organise their own individual sailing arrangements. By 1995 membership had declined and a decision made to withdraw from its affiliation to the RYA. The late Harry Ashley, Yachting Correspondent for the Bournemouth Echo for many years, wrote at the time:

> *'As a yacht club, PHYC has played a significant part in promoting Poole as a boating centre, including acting as host club to world-class events'.*

The club still continues, on a social basis, for customers of the Marina and for those who wish to retain their connection with PHYC. Members can use the hotel facilities and the administration is dealt with from the Marina Office.

Commodores between 1955 and 1995 have been:

Colonel R H Broome DSO MC	T W Murdoch Esq
Greville Humphries Esq	R V Smith Esq
Dr J Dixon Wheatcroft	J Groves Esq
R A Aldridge Esq	B Benstead Esq
H R Moore Esq	E Hall Esq
A E Nightingale Esq	

Owners for the last 30 years, the Smith family have developed the hotel into a 3-star establishment together with the 300 berth marina and a boatyard. Part of the Best Western Group, Salterns Hotel has two restaurants, three bars, 20 bedrooms, three conference/meeting rooms and a licence to hold weddings; in 1998 the AA awarded it the highest percentage rating of any hotel of its category in England. Salterns has two Red Rosettes for food with the current Executive Chef being Nigel Popperwell assisted by Head Chef David Marshall.

Run as a Family Trust, John N J Smith is Managing Director, and his wife Beverley takes an active part in the running of the hotel. A businessman from London, John Smith's father had successfully developed the Lesney Toy Company (Matchbox Cars) and wanted another business challenge away from the capital. Becoming familiar with the area through holidays at Sandbanks, they began to search locally for a suitable proposition, and stumbled across PHYC and the boatyard. Negotiations for the sale took nearly two years and the purchase was completed in 1969.

Poole Harbour Yacht Club before the new marina was built -
Blue Lagoon in background left - 1950s.
Courtesy: S. Sieger

They had intended to demolish the property in order to re-build and develop but planning permission was not forthcoming; in 1971 some land was sold to Fraternal Estates and the three blocks of flats were erected. 1999 saw the construction of Salterns Quay - twelve 3-storey town houses fronting on to the Blue Lagoon.

As mentioned earlier in this chapter, John Clark did not spend money on repairs or renewals and the property was in a bad state when the Smith family took over - windows were falling out, a water pipe had been repaired with sticky tape, and on the first floor a gas main used as a lintel. Obviously a considerable amount of money, time and effort have been needed to transform the run-down building into the luxury hotel which stands today.

It was a gradual process - the number of rooms were reduced in order to provide much larger bedrooms with en suite facilities, a restaurant added (with a further extension of a fashionable pergola for alfresco dining in 1998), the squash court turned into two rooms, conference/meeting rooms made available, Shellies Bistro formed and the kitchens extended. A licence to hold civil marriage ceremonies was granted in 1997.

The exceptional position of the hotel has attracted many 'stars' to its doors over the years; recently the television programme 'Blind Date ' selected it as a venue for their prizewinners, and Hugh Scully with his 'Antiques Roadshow' team stayed at Salterns whilst recording their programme in Poole.

The Smith family have also continued to improve the berthing and mooring facilities since they acquired the site in 1969. On 24th July 1974 (a plaque exists to commemmorate the occasion) Sir Alec Rose officially opened the new Salterns Marina - it was a splendid event with 300 guests and the Band of the Royal Marines in attendance.

Awarded five 'Gold Anchors' by the Yacht Harbour Association in 1998, Salterns Marina offers 75 swinging moorings with free launch service, 300 alongside berths on floating pontoons with access to fresh water and electricity, excellent adjacent toilet and shower facilities, a travelling hoist which can lift boats up to 45 tonnes and 20 metres in length, heated purpose-built boatshed, a five-tonne gantry hoist, 24-hour service for petrol, gas and diesel and long or short-term storage ashore.

Aerial View - early 1970s
Salterns Marina in foreground, Blue Lagoon to left
Courtesy: Philip Smith

Salterns Hotel/PHYC 1999

CHAPTER SIX
EAST DORSET SAILING CLUB

Situated at the foot of Evening Hill and by Whitley Lake is Poole Harbour's oldest and smallest sailing club. There was, at one time, some controversy regarding the year in which East Dorset Sailing Club (EDSC) was established, and although 1897 appears in Lloyd's Register of Yachts, it is generally accepted that the Club began in 1875. The founding father was Mr F J B Beckford; he served the Club for 47 years and lived on Evening Hill (known then as Lilliput Hill Road) in a house called 'Witley' at the corner with Crichel Mount Road.

In the beginning there was just a short pier/landing stage. This was the cause of a spot of bother with Lord Wimborne whose agent, Mr C Paterson, wrote the following letter to Mr Beckford on 13th April 1892:

> *'I observe that a pier for boats has recently been built opposite Flag Farm Estate Parkstone, and upon making enquiry received your name and address as one of the parties concerned in it.*
> *As the pier has been built upon Lord Wimborne's land and without his sanction, I must ask you to remove it within one week from this date or pay an acknowledgment of £1. a year'.*

In reply Mr Beckford stated that those who subscribed to erect the boat jetty were unaware that any portion of it was built on land belonging to Lord Wimborne, and he proceeded to offer His Lordship half a crown (2/6d or 12$\frac{1}{2}$p) only, which in fact was accepted.

However, the matter did not run smoothly for someone had told the pier committee that the particular piece of foreshore did not belong to Lord Wimborne anyway, and they withheld the rent which rather upset the Agent. He wrote 'pay up or we shall demolish the pier' and a week later 'pay up within a week or the rent will be made £5.' No further records exist regarding the pier problem nor do the accounts show any payment having been made. Seemingly, Mr Beckford and his colleagues decided to get on with their sailing activities, with no further thought to Lord Wimborne.

Also in 1892 Mr Beckford made a request to the Trustees of the Quays of Poole to deepen the channel from his pier to the Whitley Lake, and received a reply telling him that it was not their custom to allow dredgers to be used for private purposes. He was evidently used to getting his own way, and wrote back saying that their decision was entirely unacceptable - my proposal would be an improvement to the harbour and of benefit to the Borough'; he received a promise from the Borough Surveyor to draw up plans for a pier 20 feet longer than that originally envisaged, together with a new slipway. This work was carried out by Poole Corporation in 1895 when the sea wall around the harbour was built, thus enclosing EDSC, together with the promised slipway.

The very early Minute Books of the Club have not survived and the first recorded Minutes of a meeting on 18th December 1896 refer to 'The Proceedings of the Pier Committee' - the six present being Mr F J B Beckford (Chairman and Secretary), Mr H Forde, Colonel Everett, Mr J H Slade, Mr G Peck and Major Webb. It seems that the annual subscription of one guinea (£1.05p) was set on that occasion.

From the accounts in 1897 we learn that £41.00. was paid to a Mr Guy for the first extension to the pier, a new hackboat purchased for £7.00., a pair of rowlocks for 2s.0d. (10p) and two notice boards for 11s.1d. (55p). At a meeting in 1898 the Committee decided to employ a Pier Man at 15s.0d. (75p) weekly and the accounts show that he was provided with a jersey at 11s.6d. (57½p) together with a cap at 2s.6d. (12½p). A resolve was made to 'make representation to Bournemouth Steamboat Company as to the inconvenient and dangerous speed at which their steamers proceed up and down the harbour'.

At some stage permission had been granted from the Board of Trade to extend their pier into tidal waters and this was done for a length of 283 feet to reach the north side of Whitley Lake; a small shelter was then built for the Pier Man. This was the first reference to any building, but in 1902 it was resolved to appoint a committee for the design of a 16 x 10 foot cycle shed, the estimate for which was £15.00. A rough sketch of the design bears some resemblance to the corrugated iron building which was replaced in 1969.

Although no mention is made of it in any of the Minute Books, old letters indicate that there was a conflict between the subscribing members and the general public over the use of the slipway, which had been built with public funds in 1895. The Town Clerk referred to permission to build a fence in April 1904 and wrote 'The Council will give such permission, subject to the payment of one shilling per annum, and an undertaking being given to remove the fence at any time when called upon'. The fence was erected and the following year the committee were told to remove it as complaints had been received saying that the public were unable to use the slipway. No further problems appear to have occurred until 1912 when the Club issued a summons against two men who had broken down the fence, but they were not convicted.

In 1914 there were 19 members of the EDSC paying the full subscription of two guineas (£2.l0p) and seven with a pier membership of half that sum. Silence then prevails for the duration of World War One (1914-1918).

Minutes of committee meetings resumed in 1919 with Mr F J B Beckford still heading the list of those present; his name is still to the fore in 1922 but not after that year, and by 1925 Mr H J Sykes was Commodore.

1933 saw the occurrence of an event rare in yachting circles as Mrs F Sherston was elected as Lady Commodore. Widow of Colonel Sherston, who had been Secretary in the earlier years, she accepted the office knowing that the Club was in danger of disintegrating. Through low membership, and expenses that could not be met, an overdraft had been incurred and they were faced with the prospect of trying to get another. Mrs Sherston called a special meeting and the Minutes record that not only was it decided to keep the Club running but also that all present agreed to assist with a donation of £3.l0.0d. each (£3.50p) to cover the deficit. These efforts were obviously successful for a small credit was apparent in 1934. Mrs Sherston died soon after resigning as Commodore in 1935.

It is indeed rare for yacht clubs to appoint Lady Commodores and this possibly did not occur again within the Harbour sailing clubs until February 1999 when Mrs Mary Reddyhoff was appointed Lady Commodore of Parkstone Yacht Club, the first in its 104 year history.

1937 was an important year for EDSC. Mr H J Sykes was once again Commodore, and at long last the Club signed an agreement with Lord Wimborne for the purchase of their site on payment of £33.4.6d. (£33.25p); it had taken 62 years to achieve possession of their own foundations. The money was again raised by donation, and even after paying for storm damage repairs to 85 yards of the pier, there was a deficit of only l5s.0d. (75p).

The Club now seemed to be on an even keel, but yet again war intervened and nothing happened at EDSC for the six years of World War II (1939-1945). Poole Harbour was used for the BOAC Flying Boats from 1939 and the run-up to D-Day in June 1944, surrounding houses and hotels taken over for use by the Services and everyone was either serving in the Forces or doing essential civilian war work.

The flag was hoisted again in 1945 and the first task of the Commodore, Mr Percy Woodcock, famous yachting author and Yachting Monthly correspondent, was to convene a special meeting to assess the cost of replacing the pier which had to be totally dismantled, and to put in the necessary claim to the War Office. A sum of £1274.7s.8d. (£1274.37p) was agreed and in 1947 the pier was rebuilt. Its opening marked the beginning of a period in which the Club no longer needed to seek new members, nor struggle for its rights of tenure. By 1948 the membership had doubled and the Club's title to property at Whitley Pier entered at His Majesty's Land Registry.

Captain George Stead was Commodore in 1969 when the old Club premises were demolished and replaced with a solid brick built Clubhouse. It was a single storey building with a 'top deck' approached by an outside stairway, which was ideal for picnics, sunbathing and watching the ever-changing yachting scene. The new building was formally opened by Mrs Marjorie C Stead on 21st June 1969. The guest of honour, Alderman A Lloyd Allen JP Mayor of Poole, arrived by sea and was piped aboard by Philip Okey, a 1st Lilliput Sea Scout. Later becoming Commodore in 1999, he is the first son in the history of EDSC to follow in his father's footsteps. A plaque, designed and executed by Mr Bernard Charles, was set into the wall near the main door to mark the opening of the new building, but the lettering is now difficult to read.

The builders were H R Briggs of Bournemouth, who demolished the old premises on 1st March and finished the new building on time by 31st May 1969. The architect, Mr D Hills, was a Club member and the design is such that it blends and disappears into the background remarkably well. This same structure still stands today but with another storey, the Brownsea Room, which was opened on 9th February 1992 by the then Commodore, Mr H W Noakes. In keeping with the traditions of the Club, both the 1969 building and this 1994 addition were financed from their own resources. 'No outside financial help has ever been sought, which in view of the small membership, particularly in the early years, is something to be proud of'.

In 1975 two officers of the EDSC, Mr Harold C W Geach and Mr Leslie G L Lees, produced a Centenary booklet on the history of the Club and it is the information in that publication that has enabled me to write this chapter. The sailing activities of the Club take up the last few pages in that history, and we learn that whilst these were always on a 'do your own thing' basis, competitive sailing emerged in 1948. Colonel Bersey, then Commodore of the Royal Motor Yacht Club, had written to other clubs in the harbour - Hamworthy and Bournemouth Sailing Club (later to become Poole Yacht Club), Parkstone Yacht Club and East Dorset Sailing Club - inviting them to send representatives to a meeting at the Royal Motor Yacht Club in the autumn of 1947. (Poole Harbour Yacht Club did not come into the picture until 1949). This resulted in a 6-day Regatta, sponsored by the four clubs and supported by the Corporations of Poole and

Bournemouth and the Harbour Commissioners. Under the name of 'The Poole and Bournemouth Yachting Week' it was held 28th June to 3rd July 1948, and was so successful it became an annual event; gradually changing its sponsorship and character it later became known as 'Poole Week'. Still an annual event, Parkstone Yacht Club are now solely responsible for running it, and have done so since 1956.

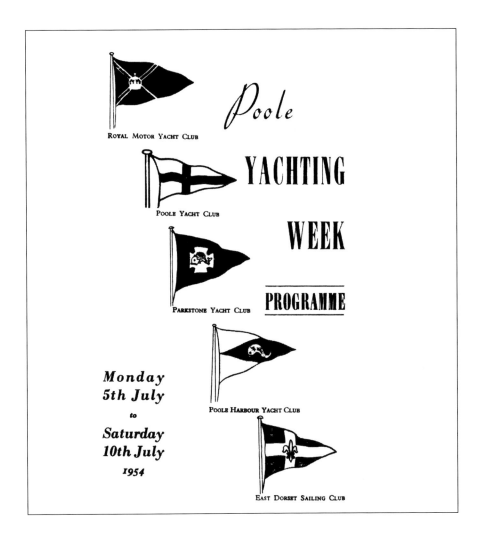

The EDSC representatives at that first meeting in 1947 were Mr Percy Woodcock Commodore, Mr Guy Emerson Secretary and Mr J G Robinson; and it was decided that the day's racing should be run under the burgee of the Club allocated for that day. There was, it seems, some controversy regarding the levy from each Club towards the preliminary expenses but this was eventually resolved; and EDSC provided a Silver Challenge Cup inscribed 'Poole and Bournemouth Regatta'. This Cup was later returned and became the Trophy for the Club's Cruiser Race.

At that first Regatta the EDSC 'day' was 29th June and was 'celebrated in fine style with a Garden Party from 4.00 - 6.00 pm at Shore Lodge at the invitation of Colonel H J Finer and his wife'. The following year the Garden Party was once again held at Shore Lodge (Colonel Finer was then Rear Commodore) on 5th July, and it is recorded that 200 guests attended. It turned out to be the last such event, for Colonel Finer and his family left Shore Lodge to live in South Africa.

Following the election in 1951 of the Club's first Sailing Secretary, Mr J G Robinson, a Challenge Cup was given by Major Douglas Milne for 'a centreboard dinghy race round Bulpit Beacon'. The event at the end of August that year was a great success, and included a Challenge Cup for a power boat race provided by the new Sailing Secretary. Named 'The Regatette' it continued to take place for many years. Mr J G Robinson eventually served the Club for 16 years in dual roles, first as Rear Commodore/Sailing Secretary, then as Commodore/Sailing Secretary and subsequently as President/Sailing Secretary until he died during the 1967 season.

He was followed as Sailing Secretary in 1968 by Mr Bernard Charles, who carried on the tradition of 'The Regatette' as well as organising other sailing events. When Ken Latham produced the 'Poole Sprat', Mr Charles encouraged youngsters to learn to sail and arranged a 'Sprat Week' during which sailing tuition was given. This resulted in many 'Sprats' taking part in subsequent Junior Dinghy Races. Mr Bernard Charles was also responsible for laying on the Club's first ever Cruiser Race.

One of the authors of the Centenary Booklet, Mr Leslie G L Lees, took over as Sailing Secretary in 1970. 'As the Sailing Cruiser Fleet had grown considerably we decided to make the Club Cruiser Race an annual event and learn to stage it on our own. A very experienced Race Officer from Parkstone Yacht Club, Mr Tipple, kindly agreed to help us and to train some of our members in the necessary procedures'.

Over a course in Poole Bay, the Cruiser event proved increasingly popular, and since a Club member gave an antique Candelabra as a sailing trophy, it became known as 'The Candelabra Trophy Race'. Mr Lees was succeeded as Sailing Secretary by Mr Ken Okey in 1973.

Until 1946, the small membership made it possible to hold committee meetings in private homes, but as numbers increased it became necessary to use local hotels for AGM's and social functions. Venues for dinners and Cocktail parties were the Sandbanks Hotel, Branksome Court Hotel (demolished), Branksome Tower Hotel (demolished) and Harbour Heights Hotel (planning application 1999 to demolish)! It seems that in those days 'a good dinner at a luxury hotel cost members 12/6d (62½p) each, and out of that we could pay for Club guests'.

The building of the new Clubhouse in 1969 meant that the Club has been able to hold all the necessary meetings and most functions on their own premises.

EDSC is now mainly a Cruisers Club with sailing in the Solent and across to France. With an age range from seven to seventy, the Club is family orientated and Friday evenings are reserved for the young dinghy sailors. With just under 100 members in 1999, the subscription for full membership is £44.50. and Joint Membership £66.00.

LIST OF COMMODORES

1875-1925	F J B Beckford Esq	1971-1973	J N Grange-Bennett Esq
1925-1932	H J Sykes Esq	1973-1977	L G L Lees Esq
1932-1933	R Young Esq	1977-1980	D G Moore Esq
1933-1935	Mrs F Sherston	1980-1983	K H Okey Esq
1935-1938	H J Sykes Esq	1983-1986	W R German Esq
1938-1947	Sir W G Verdon-Smith	1986-1989	A C H Wood Esq
1947-1956	P Woodcock Esq	1989-1993	H W Noakes Esq
1956-1959	J G Robinson Esq	1993-1996	A R C Tatham Esq
1959-1962	A F Burt Esq	1996-1999	D F Collins Esq
1962-1971	Captain G G Stead	1999-	P M Okey Esq

The thriving Lilliput Sailing Club is based at the Blue Lagoon along Sandbanks Road. Founded by Roy Humphry in 1956, the Club's first home was at Lilliput Yacht Station where a very small hut was rented for £10.00 a year. A 'menagerie' group they were initially referred to as 'that scruffy crowd from Pizey's boatyard'; but now take their rightful place among the older harbour sailing clubs.

I have not been able to determine why the Blue Lagoon is so called - with clay at the bottom could it once have been similar to the Blue Pool near Wareham? Or perhaps the name was just an early example of 'media hype'. Originally part of 'The Salterns' as described in the chapter on Salterns Hotel and Marina, it seems probable that at some stage clay was dug out providing a uniform depth overall. It is not known when the lagoon was sealed off from the harbour although a date in the early 1900s has been suggested; sluice gates were constructed, the design of which enabled the tide to flow inwards but an outgoing tide firmly closed them.

Lilliput Sailing Club/Blue Lagoon 1999
The small gap to the right of the entrance is site of old sluice gates.
Brownsea Island in background.

By the mid-1930s the lagoon was certainly in regular use for sailing with a fleet of boats for hire, run by the Lagoon Club. The depth of water was controlled by the sluice gates, and some local folk remember it as being run on a similar basis to the boating lake in Poole Park. Still to be seen is the small gap which was the site of the sluice gates - looking out from the Clubhouse this space can be seen to the right of the entrance.

During World War II Poole was a target for the German bombers, not least because of the flying boats in the harbour and BOAC headquarters at, what is now, Salterns Hotel. In the course of a raid in 1940 a stick of bombs fell in a line from Parkstone Yacht Club - luckily the terminal building was missed, but one bomb struck the harbour wall enclosing the lagoon and let in the sea.

Apparently the lagoon residents attempted to repair the breach and hired Jack Peate for that purpose, although his strenuous efforts with two steel 12' mooring pontoons were to no avail. He eventually became a member of the Lilliput Sailing Club, hence the Jack Peate Trophy for the Lions Race.

In 1997 Alan E Heron, President of the Lilliput Sailing Club since 1990, published the History of the Club and I appreciate his courtesy in allowing me to use information from his book. The History was a compilation of his own personal recollections together with valuable sources of information from the Bournemouth Evening Echo (now the Daily Echo) written by Harry Ashley, who died in 1997. Writing under the by-line 'Leo', Harry Ashley was Yachting Correspondent for the local paper for a considerable number of years.

In 1956 businessman Roy Humphry moved to Poole from Bristol, and one afternoon walked into Harry Ashley's office demanding to see 'the chap who writes about yachting'. It seemed that his intention was to start a 'menagerie' sailing club in the harbour, a fun club where everyone could enjoy being on the water and members would be invited to sail against each other on handicap. That meeting was the start of a long friendship between the two men, and Harry Ashley eventually became the Club's first Honorary Life Member.

Roy was co-owner of a coffee bar on Poole Hill in Bournemouth, and this was the venue for the group of people who met and agreed to form a club and call it Lilliput. The new club was soon up and running in their base at Pizey's yard, with the majority of the cruisers in the 18' to 20' category and a wide variety of dinghies. A burgee was devised by Roy Humphry - a yellow ground with the letter 'L' inset in yellow inside a blue circle and two blue bars in the fly. These blue bars (bars sinister in heraldic terms, the mark of illegitimacy) were intended as a gentle joke.

Other users of Pizey's yard included keen members of the Royal Electrical and Mechanical Engineers from Blandford and the Army Sailing Association at Bovington; these two organisations soon became fully integrated into the new Lilliput Sailing Club. The Beehive Hotel was the centre of the Club's social activities in those days, and the connection is commemorated with the 'Beehive Trophy' which was presented to the Club by Mrs Nora Adamson who was licensee of the Beehive from 1943-1971.

As the Club began to flourish in the early 1960s the pressure of space became apparent. Not only was car parking space restricted with Dorset Lake Avenue becoming cluttered, but the lady living next door to Pizey's yard was not happy when members of the Club began to congregate noisily on the beach at the bottom of her garden!

So began the task of finding a new home, bearing in mind that at this early stage the Club had virtually no money available, with the subscriptions having only recently risen to £1.00 per head from its initial fee of 5s.0d (25p). Among the sites considered were the old pier opposite Rockley Point, a beach site near the Royal Marines base at Hamworthy, a public slip at Baiter and one at Salterns (this would have been before the present marina and flats were constructed). For various reasons, and in some cases objections from the local residents, none of these sites were deemed suitable.

At this stage the Blue Lagoon Marine Club came into the picture. A licensed proprietary social club with a faintly marine flavour, there was a swimming pool, lawn and patio and the building (now housing Parkway Marine) contained two club rooms, a bar, kitchen and ample changing facilities. The remainder of the site, which is now the Club's car and boat park, was mainly a tangled marshy wilderness separated from the lagoon by a free-standing concrete wall. In addition there was a 20' x 30' wooden hut and this became available for the Lilliput Sailing Club.

The Blue Lagoon Marine Club is believed to have existed before World War II when boats were for hire on the lagoon, and in the early 1960s it was owned by Alderman Geoffrey Bravery, a well-respected ex-mayor of Poole who lived in Marina Drive on the opposite side of Sandbanks Road.

By the time the Lilliput Sailing Club appeared on the scene the Blue Lagoon Club was not exactly thriving, so the arrangement whereby all members of the sailing club joined the Blue Lagoon Club and given the use of the hut and the rest of the area, was quite satisfactory to all concerned. The members then set about reclaiming the marshy wilderness - a suitable base was constructed, the present slipway prepared and a smooth surface made for the boat trolleys. At that time there was no great pressure on space and lift in/out of the cruisers was carried out with a little mobile crane known as an 'Iron Fairy'.

Eventually the Blue Lagoon Marine Club ceased to exist and in due time, after much negotiation, Lilliput Sailing Club bought the land on which the Clubhouse and Boat Park now stand. The foundation stone for the Clubhouse was laid by Roy Humphry in 1965 and much of the building work and fitting out was done by the members themselves; with finance being found through a system of £25 debentures taken out by many members. These entitled the holder to a one guinea (£1.05p) reduction in the annual subscription. The Clubhouse was completed and in use by 1966 and was formally opened on 10th December by Sir Gordon Smith, a leading helmsman of the day.

When Lilliput Sailing Club first arrived at the Blue Lagoon a priority was to improve the access from the harbour since passage was only then possible for a dinghy at high water with the plate up. The unsuccessful attempt by Jack Peate to block the gap created by the German bomb had left the two pontoons stuck at an inconvenient angle. Happily, the Army came to the rescue with a Scammel tank recovery vehicle from Bovington Camp. Under the guise of a week-end exercise, the Army and Lilliput Sailing Club members spent two days moving the pontoons.

Despite this clearance of the entrance, the water flow had only marginally improved. The Army suggested laying a chain of small explosive charges to further encourage the water flow, but it was not a popular idea with the local residents or with the Harbour Commissioners; eventually after considerable lobbying and with the whole-hearted support of Poole Yachting Association, the Commissioners themselves took on the project. It was accomplished under a youth labour scheme, using gabions filled with graded stone.

The Club continued to improve the facilities in the lagoon over the years and in 1991 an agreement was reached whereby the National Rivers Authority excavated 61 ten-ton loads of muddy clay which was used by the NRA to repair river banks in Wareham. The overall depth of the lagoon and the depth of the channels was not a nuisance in the early days with the small craft then used by the members, but it may continue to be a problem with the ever increasing dimensions of current boats.

In 1974 Roy Humphry, founder of the Lilliput Sailing Club retired as Commodore, a position he had held for 16 years. At the annual dinner in the Bournemouth Pavilion, attended by 250 members, Roy was installed formally as Founder Commodore and presented with a commemorative salver, a set of luggage and a return air fare to the USA so that he could visit his family there. He remained active in the Club until his death in 1982. All the Club members agreed that a form of memorial should be established, and a proposal to fund a new launch was the most appropriate and practicable. The 'Roy Humphry' was officially named by his wife Doris at the AGM in 1984.

As described at the beginning of this chapter Lilliput Sailing Club started as a menagerie club for all types of dinghies with, no doubt, the first concern being that of acquiring a reasonable number of members. Whereas the older harbour sailing clubs were available for particular classes, the new Club welcomed everyone with open arms and was quite prepared to arrange class racing where numbers of a particular boat made a viable fleet. This led to the appearance in Poole of a wide range of classes, one being the OK dinghies at Lilliput in 1959 with an Open Race, and subsequently the 1961 Open Meeting which attracted 20 entries from different parts of the country.

1961 was a successful year for not only was it the year in which the Club moved to the Blue Lagoon but there was a vigorous and varied racing programme. The regatta attracted a record of 130 boats, the Admirals Cup was inaugurated for team racing, the Bristol Trophy was sailed by 31 boats to Bournemouth Pier and back, the Westminster Bank presented a handsome candelabra for the first ever harbour Boxing Day race, for which 30 boats entered, and Harry Poole launched the Poole AB - a new design to teach youngsters to sail.

1962 saw the formation of the Poole Bay Olympic Sailing Association with the 5.5m World Championships staged in the Bay under the burgee of the Royal Motor Yacht Club. A number of Lilliput Sailing Club members volunteered to help and the Club widely entertained the Russian Olympic Team, who subsequently invited them to send a team to the Black Sea regatta. Unfortunately the Club were unable to accept this invitation, which included an offer of boats and accommodation.

Events over the next few years included the Army Sailing Championships, the National Championships for Shearwater Catamarans, National Solos and Wayfarers, an open race for Flying Dutchmen, an unusual event - 'Round the Wight by Night', and in 1966 the adoption of a new class, The Seafly.

At the same time as this activity in dinghies, there was a growing interest in cruiser racing, and initially the fleet was largely composed of 20' or thereabouts of bilge keel boats such as Silhouette, Vivacity and Alacrity. There were, however, some larger craft, notably 'Fireflame', a Scandinavian built boat designed by Bjarne Aas - launched in 1939 and owned by Eric Timson and Arthur Baker. Another vessel of some note was 'Cossar' owned by the Roberts family; believed to have been designed by a local man, Walter Rayner, it was built around 1936.

Regular cruiser rallies began to take place, not only to local ports, but most enthusiastically to Cherbourg where dinners were held for up to 30 members.

Lilliput Sailing Club has enjoyed a number of affiliations over the years, starting with the then Blandford based Royal Electrical and Mechanical Engineers Yacht Club, and continuing with the Army Sailing Association - between them owning a sizeable fleet of a dozen dinghies mainly GP 14's, Fireflies, Albacores and Enterprises. When the Royal Electrical and Mechanical Engineers depot at Blandford closed down in 1960 their accommodation in the Clubhouse was taken over by the 30th Signal Regiment Royal Signals, who became affiliated to Lilliput Sailing Club.

Another affiliation was that of the John Laing Sailing Club (construction company); but of particular interest is the connection with the Westminster Bank (now NatWest). In the 1960s the bank paid a block fee both for membership and parking of its boats, and continued for many years to actively support the Club. Brian Cooke was deputy manager of the Lower Parkstone branch in Commercial Road and became a dedicated member of both Lilliput Sailing Club and the NatWest Sailing Club, eventually becoming interested in single handed racing.

The great challenge then was the single handed Transatlantic Race which the exploits of 'Blondie' Haslar had brought into the public imagination. In 1968 Brian Cooke, in his boat 'Opus', took part in the Race and completed the crossing in 34 days to finish in sixth place. A painting of 'Opus' hangs in the Clubhouse. As a heavily built yacht of the old style it was not suitable to compete against the more modern boats which began to participate in these races and the Bank, clearly appreciative of the publicity value of his deeds, chartered 'British Steel' for him; Brian Cooke finished the 1972 Transatlantic Race fourth in a time of 24 days.

Together with another Lilliput/NatWest member, Brian Jensen, he took part in the Round Britain Race with a 49' trimaran 'Triple Arrow'. Despite a nasty set back at one point, they accomplished the Race finishing in 21 days, eighth out of 60 entries - 20 of whom failed to complete. His next goal for 'Triple Arrow' was the 1976 Transatlantic Race and as part of his build-up for this event Brian decided to try and break a long-standing record for single-handed sailors by covering 4000 miles in under 20 days. This was a target which had previously eluded Sir Francis Chichester in a monohull.

Brian set off from Plymouth in December 1975 intending to cross the Atlantic by the southern route. His last contact was on 11th December when he was becalmed 700 miles from the Canary Islands, and nothing more was heard. An extensive air and sea search eventually found

'Triple Arrow' upside down about 500 miles west of the Canaries, apparently undamaged and complete with life raft and all sails set. It seemed most likely that Brian Cooke had fallen overboard and the boat sailed on without him, and was subsequently flipped over by increasing winds. It was impractical to salvage the boat and 'Triple Arrow' drifted across the Atlantic and was wrecked in the West Indies. This sailing tragedy was all the more poignant as Brian had intended the 1976 Transatlantic Race to be his final effort in competitive sailing, and he was at the time occupied in fitting out a 33' monohull for his own use in retirement.

COMMODORES

1956-1974	R M Humphry Esq	1987-1990	G K Gwinnett Esq
1974-1976	R Parker Esq	1990-1993	W R German Esq
1976-1979	A C Baker Esq	1993-1994	P I Barr Esq
1979-1984	A E Heron Esq	1994-1997	T R Barnes Esq
1984-1987	R G Carter Esq	1997-	G Wall Esq

PRESIDENTS

1955-1958	P Nicol Esq	1968-1990	F L Shergold Esq
1958-1960	W Remington Esq	1990-	A E Heron Esq
1960-1968	G Ward Esq		

CHAPTER EIGHT

LILLIPUT YACHT STATION/PIZEY'S YARD

Pizey's Boatyard, or to use its correct title, Lilliput Yacht Station, goes back to 12th May 1927. That is the date on which a piece of land running down to the harbour's edge was bought from Lord Wimborne by a Mrs Ellen Josephine May Knight. On Sandbanks Road opposite Heathside (now Avalon), it became Knights Yacht Services at the Woodside Boatyard. Wimborne Estate covenants did not allow a school or a soap factory to be built on the land, but it seems that a boatyard was deemed a suitable trade! Mrs Knight initially lived in a caravan on the site and her son, believed to be Joseph R H Knight (known as Bob), and his French wife ran the boatyard, living next door at 326 Sandbanks Road. Using his bum-boat Bob Knight would deliver the morning papers, water and provisions to the moored yachts during the summers prior to World War II.

Mrs Knight sold the business in January 1948 to a Mr Horace W Clark, who by then was living in the next door bungalow (now a small block of flats). Not keeping it for very long Mr Clark sold the yard to Mr Royston Dudley George Pizey DFC at the end of 1949. Hailing from Chingford in Essex (where there had been a long standing family business at nearby Leytonstone) Royston Pizey served in both World Wars (1914-1918 and 1939-1945), and was a keen amateur motor yachtsman with a dream of offering 'a complete service to the yachtsman'. He ran the business until 1965 when the property was transferred to his son, Kenneth Dudley Pizey, who then continued until he himself retired in September 1988.

In the early days boat owners needed someone to prepare their craft for them so that when they came down for their week-end of sailing everything would be 'ready to go', and this was one of the services offered by the Lilliput Yacht Station. Royston Pizey also supplied a 'boatman service' to the East Dorset Sailing Club at the time when Mr Percy Woodcock, yachting author and 'Yachting Monthly' correspondent, was Commodore. His first long-standing customer, with his sloop 'Mary Jean', was Captain George Stead Commodore of EDSC in 1969 and father of George Stead, a former director of Southern Ocean Shipyard based on the Hamworthy side of Poole Quay. George Stead crewed for Ted Heath in one of his 'Morning Cloud' yachts; and his grandson Adrian has followed in the family footsteps, skippering a successful British boat in the recent Admiral's Cup.

In 1954 Royston Pizey supported the establishment of Lilliput Sailing Club by Roy Humphry and provided accommodation for them until they moved to their new Clubhouse at the Blue Lagoon in 1966. In the beginning, it seems that the Lilliput Sailing Club was described as 'the scruffy crowd from Pizey's yard', but subsequently took their rightful place with the older harbour clubs.

Ken Pizey followed Percy Woodcock as 'Yachting Monthly' correspondent and carried on this task for over 25 years. He joined his father at Lilliput Yacht Station in 1951 after serving in the Merchant Navy and the Royal Signals, and working as a civilian for the Ordnance Survey in various parts of the country. Ken built upon the reputation his father had achieved and in order to consolidate the financial position he increased the number of moorings to 162, played down the repair side and sub-let the brokerage and chandlery.

Lilliput Yacht Station covered in snow
Courtesy: Ken Pizey

The boatyard provided an essential service for yachtsmen and was not into building boats, although Ken Pizey did make his own 'Flying Fifteens'. Space was at a premium and none of the sheds were large enough to accommodate boat building.

Leasing the ground floor offices of the main building from the Pizey family in 1954, Lilliput Yacht Station was the first Poole home for John Threlfall's South Western Marine Factors before they moved to larger premises in Pottery Road and later to the Nuffield Estate.

Ken Pizey has memories of many interesting and eccentric characters who used Pizey's Yard, but one person he remembers with great respect is Commander Claude Woollard, Master Mariner and member of the Cape Horners Society, who lived at Even Keel 1 Dorset Lake Avenue. Serving in the Royal Naval Reserve during the First World War, Commander Woollard was in charge of troopships running from Marseilles; he supported the local Sea Cadets and ran a Girls Nautical Training Scheme. His large sailing vessels, including the 'English Rose' were moored over by Brownsea and even in his 80's he was still actively involved with the Nautical Training Scheme.

Amongst others remembered by Ken Pizey is Mrs Aubrey, a keen motor yachtswoman who lived at Arne Cliff, then the last house on Evening Hill, Mr C J Carey-Wood and his yacht 'Elizabeth Jim' who lived at Dilkush in Gardens Crescent and Major Arthur N Butler (once a Poole Mayor and Sheriff), whose family ran department stores in Poole and Wimborne.

Also remembered is an interesting 16 mm film shot by the Reverend Brian Hession, who had a house in Nairn Road and spent one summer living in a cottage on the other side of the harbour. Entitled 'A Message from Goathorn' the film featured the surrounding countryside and included footage of the water postman who delivered the mail to all the islands in Poole Harbour; it is believed that it was shown at Parkstone Yacht Club. If this film still exists and is in good condition, it would make very interesting viewing.

As with any other business, running a yacht station is not all 'plain sailing'. In the 1980s Truckline tore up some of the moorings and it was two years before the matter was satisfactorily sorted out.

The great gale in October 1987 was almost a disaster, or so it seemed to Ken Pizey when he first set eyes on the devastation the next morning. The 620' pier was broken in three places and sunken boats were to be seen in all directions. Through sheer hard work he managed to have everything almost back to normal for the start of the next season. It was this experience which suggested to Ken that he might give thought to retirement!

Soon after the gale, a bait digger from Southampton trod on a spike as he made his way under the wrecked pier. He did not approach Ken Pizey directly but subsequently sued Lilliput Yacht Station for the cost of a pair of boots and socks plus a week's wages, being unfit for work. The claim did not run smoothly and was still proceeding a year or two later, the compensation figure having mysteriously escalated during that time.

When the boatyard was sold in 1988, the new owners put in a planning application to develop the site and build six luxury flats. There was a public enquiry, and to Ken's amusement, many of his ex-customers formed a protest movement 'Save Pizey's Boatyard', to persuade Poole Borough Council that it was a local amenity which should not disappear. The planning application was not successful, and the boatyard eventually passed into new ownership.

CHAPTER NINE

THE BEEHIVE

This early photograph of Sandbanks Road shows the rural atmosphere
which prevailed - the horse drawn transport and one of
many oak trees which lined the road. The Beehive on right.
Courtesy: Eldridge Pope

There has been an inn on the site since the early 19thC, and the first documentation in the Eldridge Pope archives is for the sale of land from the Commissioners under the Great Canford Inclosure to John Baker. The Receipt dated 15th October 1813 is in the sum of fourteen pounds for two pieces of land in the parish of Great Canford.

It is known that in 1863 Peregrine Baker leased a dwelling house to Frederick Styring, Brewer of Poole, and later that year (confusing though it may seem) Styring re-leased 'the Inn and public house lately erected' back to Peregrine Baker! The Indenture dated 29th September 1863 names Samuel Colborne Scott of Longfleet Gentleman, John Sydenham Bookseller of Poole, Peregrine Baker of Longfleet Joiner, Thomas Woodcock of Southsea Steward in the service of the Peninsula and Oriental Company, John Woodcock of Slingsby in the county of York Corn Merchant. Mentioned in the body of this Indenture is a previous one dated 4th December 1832 with the names of Robert Henning Parr, John Baker, Richard Weston Parr and John Durant.

The Indenture dated 29th September 1863 states 'All that parcel of land no. 206A containing seven perches more or less situate at Parkstone in the county of Dorset bounded on the north east by an Ancient Road and on the south east and south west by ancient Inclosures nos 208 and 207 at a yearly rent of two pounds. A further Indenture dated 9th December 1863 advises that the Lessee 'will not sell or allow to be sold any beer, ale, porter, cider, wine, spirits, cordial or other fermented liquors other than such as shall be supplied by the Lessor without his written order, under a penalty of Five Pounds for every offence, the same to be recoverable as rent in arrear and to keep open the said premises and use the said House as an Inn and Public House and keep and conduct the same in an orderly and proper manner agreeable in all respects to the tenor and spirit of the Licence and the law for the time being regulating Public Houses'. The Witness on these two Indentures was M F Curtis, Clerk to M Kemp Welch and W Aldridge, Sols of Poole.

In 1866 or 1867 Frederick Styring apparently bought the property outright from Peregrine Baker; and in 1900 Eldridge Pope (Brewers of Dorchester) acquired the Poole (Styrings) Brewery together with the public house estate, which included The Beehive.

In the early days of The Beehive, Sandbanks Road was a narrow country lane and the property was surrounded by farmland with the saltings at the rear. Customers might then have been salt workers, farm labourers, fishermen and possibly workers in the alum and copperas industry from the Lilliput Road area. Sandbanks Road had an abundance of oak trees and a report in the local paper bemoaned the loss of a landmark - an ancient oak outside The Beehive. 'The tree is reckoned to be around 500 years old and has a trunk of noble girth, but its destruction was decided upon in the interests of safety, as there is a bend in the road at that place'. The tree was one of a number of oaks between The Beehive and the corner of the Elms Estate. An attempt to preserve them was made when Sandbanks Road was improved a few years after the First World War (1914-1918) but most disappeared, although there may be one or two preserved in private gardens.

A paragraph in the Dorset County Chronicle dated 16th February 1893 gives a different insight into the role of The Beehive:

'On Monday morning the Borough Coroner (Mr G Braxton Aldridge) held an inquest at the Beehive Inn Lilliput Parkstone concerning the death of a little boy named Willie Ross, six years of age. It seems that on Thursday last the father and mother left the house in charge of their children while they went to work. The deceased and two younger sisters were in bed suffering from colds, and a fire was kept in the bedroom. The deceased got out of bed and warmed himself by the fire. In doing so his nightgown became ignited. A neighbour hearing the unusual screams of the child was attracted to the house, and the father and mother and a doctor were sent for, but Dr McNeill did not reach the house till nearly three hours afterwards. Dr McNeill never once looked at the burns and did not give the child any medicine until Friday night. On Saturday morning the little fellow died. The jury returned a verdict that the child died through burns accidentally inflicted and added the rider that they were dissatisfied with Dr McNeill's treatment of this case'.

Since 1900 Eldridge Pope have master minded many changes - they bought more land from Lord Wimborne and in 1903 the property was rebuilt at a cost of £1710.00 by builders A & F Wilson. 1919/20 saw the addition of a new wing, more land purchased at the rear in 1923 and garages built in 1934.

An early 1930s tourist guide quotes the telephone number as Canford Cliffs 9, and indicates that 'excellent accommodation is provided at The Beehive Hotel, Sandbanks Road being the only fully licensed residential hotel along that road, and a convenient half-way house on the journey from Parkstone to Sandbanks'. Attractions on offer to would-be patrons by G S Ryall, the proprietor, were magnificent views of Poole Harbour and Brownsea Island, a grill room, putting green, delightful tea gardens, a camping site and facilities for boating, fishing and swimming.

In the early part of 1939 planning permission was granted to rebuild The Beehive even further back from the road, but the project was shelved due to the outbreak of the Second World War in the September of that year. A Poole and East Dorset Herald reporter seems to have waxed lyrical about it all on 24th May 1939 with the headline 'Beehive Will Hum With Activity. £8000.00 New Hotel Nearer Harbour'. The plan was to build a very modern structure nearer the sea with lounges and bars opening out on to a garden and the water, with furnishings in the modern roadhouse style. But 45 years were to elapse before any alterations took place.

The longest serving tenant at The Beehive, for 34 years, was Mrs Nora Adamson. Moving there in 1937 with her husband Jack, Mrs Adamson took over the licence during the war in 1943 when he was serving overseas with BOAC, and on his death in 1946 became the tenant.

To mark the occasion of her retirement in September 1971 Mrs Adamson was presented with a silver salver by the directors of Eldridge Pope. Her family had always been closely connected with the licensed trade and with Eldridge Pope in particular. Her step-father, Mr Percy Toombs, was the licensee for the South Western Hotel in Bournemouth (opposite the Central Station and now I think a nightclub) before becoming the first tenant of the newly opened Strouden Park Hotel just before the Second World War. Her brother, Mr A W Green, was at the New Bell Inn at Pokesdown and was succeeded there by his son, Alderman Michael Green.

The Beehive Hotel - July 1958
Courtesy: Eldridge Pope

Patrons of The Beehive in the early 1900s would, I feel sure, still recognise their 'local' for the exterior of the building has changed very little in that time, and unlike a number of other licensed premises in Poole, still retains its original name. One example of this change of name being the Conjuror's Half Crown (previously The Sloop) on the Civic Centre roundabout, where the local historical name has been lost.

The Beehive received a new look in 1984 when alterations and extensions were carried out. Whilst continuing to provide the traditional pub privacy for adults, family rooms were constructed overlooking the gardens; a covered patio and barbecue built and play areas created for the children. An unusual feature is the floodlit petanque, or boules pitch. At the official opening of the new 'Family Pub' in April 1984 Mr Jeremy and Mr Christopher Pope watched the then Mayor of Poole, Councillor Roger Buss, draw the first pint. A special ceremony in the gardens followed the opening when the son and daughter of Mrs Nora Adamson, who had died just before the work on The Beehive was completed, presented a garden seat in her memory.

Since 1971 The Beehive has been under management and the present managers, who have been there since 1994, are Hayley and Jeffrey Dunne.

List of Tenants at The Beehive Inn/Hotel in Sandbanks Road:

1879	William Rose	1915	Augustus C C Sharp
1881	George Frank Strickland	1923	Henry Gilmore Dodderidge
1903	Charles Edwin Miell	1927	George Stanner Ryall
1906	Alfred Butt	1937	John Adamson
1907	George Alcock	1946	Mrs Nora Adamson
1909	George Parsons		

CHAPTER TEN
WOMEN'S INSTITUTES

There are two Women's Institutes in the area and both meet each month in the Holy Angels Church Hall; Gulliver on a Monday evening and Lilliput on a Tuesday afternoon. Founded in 1897 by a Canadian mother in Stoney Cross, Ontario, the first W I in England was set up in 1915, only a short distance away - in Wallisdown.

Non-political and non-religious, all Women's Institutes are part of the National Federation, which in turn is served by the individual counties. With their headquarters in Dorchester, the Dorset Federation of Women's Institutes was formed in 1917 with 19 Institutes, and the 75th birthday celebration was held at Kingston Maurward in August 1992. Entitled 'A Bit of a Do in 92', the event was a mixture of displays from the past and for the future, competitions, music, dancing and country pursuits; Lilliput successfully entered a set piece called 'The Glorious Twelfth' gaining 91 points out of a maximum of 100.

The public image of the 'Jam and Jerusalem' ladies is now rather out of date. Indeed, they do make jam (sometimes) and they do sing Jerusalem but the wide range of activities which can be enjoyed is such that there isn't the time or the energy to participate in them all. Topical matters of international and national importance are discussed and resolutions made which are passed to the National Federation and eventually to the appropriate Government departments.

At local level there are speakers - informative, historical, light-hearted, scientific, educational and subjects of local interest. Outings include theatre visits, attractions, gardens, Buckingham Palace Apartments, factories, agricultural shows, Houses of Parliament; and within the main structure is the opportunity to join small groups on home economics, drama, crafts and singing. Members can attend County and National meetings, and Denman College in Oxfordshire provides short courses in all sorts of subjects - many members have learned a new skill through one of these courses.

Activities within the Dorset Federation again cover a wide field. Sports and Leisure include line dancing, skittles, table tennis, hot air ballooning, aqua aerobics, dinghy sailing and tournaments for whist, scrabble and bowls. Photographic, drama and art workshops come under the heading of Combined Arts, whilst International Environment and Public Affairs range from a 'Time and Motion Day', links with MAFF on 'Genetic Modification and Food', and co-ordination with The Tidy Britain Group regarding the National Spring Clean in April 1999.

Lilliput W I - 11th September 1990
21st birthday celebrations, with several members in period costume.
Courtesy: Lilliput W I

With around 100 members the Lilliput Institute, which began in 1969, has a lot of talent to choose from and three of them (Mrs Elsie Murray, Mrs Judy Hunkin, Mrs Sheila Mabon) successfully published a book to celebrate their 25th anniversary. Entitled 'Lilliput Larder 1994' it was a collection of favourite recipes abundantly illustrated with cartoon figures and with numerous 'Tip Top, Topical Tips' - hints on cooking, housekeeping and social matters e.g. 'If you want to be discreet about the number of candles on your birthday cake, place them in the form of a question mark' and 'if you want to eat less, use chopsticks or eat in front of a mirror'. So successful was the book that three reprints were necessary.

Lilliput was the largest Dorset W I in 1998, and officers for 1999 were President Mrs H Fearnley, Vice-President Mrs J Gibbs, Secretary Miss M E Ginn and Treasurer Mrs S Martin.

By the end of 1969, only a few months after its inception, Lilliput was full to capacity and had a waiting list, so another one was formed. In March 1970 45 new members enrolled at the first meeting of the Gulliver W I (later changing its name to Gulliver Evening W I). Officers elected were President Mrs B Ashby, Secretary Mrs P Saunders, Treasurer Mrs L Stubley and Press Secretary Miss Ann M Vickery who was only 19 at the time.

As with Lilliput, many and varied have been the activities recorded in the scrapbooks and the 1970s including the planting of two deciduous conifers within the grounds of the Church of the Holy Angels, giving a seat to Poole Borough Council for use at Whitecliff and participation in a pageant at Poole College to raise money for the 1977 Queen's Silver Jubilee Appeal. Collaboration with Poole Museum relating to events at Scaplens Court followed in the 1980s, and local matters were given an airing when Ian Andrews, the then Town Clerk, attended one of their meetings.

To commemorate their 25th anniversary in February 1995, Gulliver presented four wooden seats to Lilliput First School. These were made by Mr Tompkins and the scrapbook contains numerous thank you letters and drawings from the children. One was from Jonathan 'Thank you for the four lovely benches. In the summer I will sit on one, I might even try to sleep on them. They are very lovely I must say. I will read and tell jokes on them'.

The W I seemed to receive plenty of press coverage in the early years, but on occasions reporters could not resist referring to the 'little people' or the 'Lilliputians'! One even confused the W I and Townswomen's Guild, alluding to Gulliver Evening Townswomen's Institute.

Gulliver W I currently have 70 members, and the officers for 1999 were President Mrs J Smith, Vice-President Mrs F Godsell, Registrar Mrs D Harvey and Treasurer Mrs E Crook.

1995. Gulliver W I - presentation of the benches,
made by Mr Tompkins, to Lilliput First School.
Courtesy: Gulliver W I

CHAPTER ELEVEN

HOUSES

SALTERNS HOUSE

With thirteen grandfather clocks inside the house and fourteen wells within the grounds, Salterns House, off Brownsea View Avenue, held happy childhood memories for Mary Butts author of 'The Crystal Cabinet' which was published in 1937 just after her death at the age of 46.

Her father, Captain Frederick John Butts bought the property (believed to have stood in 100 acres) in 1861 after distinguished service in the Crimean War. In her book, his daughter says that he acquired the house because 'you could walk down to bathe in the open sea, a matter of three miles, in your nightshirt'.

Mary Butts wrote of 'walking a mile to a day school in the Parkstone woods, and of walking down the drive and through the fields to the pillar box by the bottom lodge'. She did not enjoy their trips into Bournemouth 'where you had to wear best clothes always, where Daddy went to a Club and Mother to shops or to pay awful calls'.

The title of her book 'The Crystal Cabinet' is taken from William Blake's poem of the same name; the connection came through her grandfather, Thomas Butts, who was a patron and friend of William Blake. Salterns House at one time contained 42 of his paintings, many of which are now in The Tate Gallery

In 1890 the adjoining cream coloured three storey property 'Whiteladies' on Anthonys Avenue was built as a library and a gallery to house these paintings, and was linked to Salterns House. 'Whiteladies' was turned into flats in 1946, and permission was granted in 1999 for this property to be demolished and the land used for flat redevelopment. Confusion arose at that time because many local people believed that Salterns House itself was the property to be demolished.

Salterns House is not a listed building since so many alterations have been made over the years; it is now divided into two flats. In 1991 it was for sale through the estate agents Goadsby and Harding and was described as one of the first substantial houses to be built in the Lilliput area - the particulars indicated three reception rooms (including the 20' drawing room with oak panelled walls), four bedrooms and two bathrooms, together with a Victorian conservatory containing an 80 year old grapevine.

It was Captain F J Butts who gave the land on which the Church of the Holy Angels is built, and in her book Mary Butts indicates that this was in memory of her father's son, from a previous marriage, who had died at the age of 22.

Salterns House - 1998

Her descriptions of the area surrounding Salterns House make interesting reading - Viney's Farm, Witt's Farm, Bryant's Wood, Sandy Lane, the heathland, waterworks and reservoirs, the clay pits and the potteries - 'a coarse industry - drain pipes and bricks' (George Jennings South Western Pottery) and the short cut to the village of Lilliput with its single shop (the old Post Office and general stores in Lilliput Road). Mention is made of early inhabitants and the quiet gentry who had made their homes in the area - Mrs Watkins at Lilliput House, Mrs Dawson-Damer at The Elms and the Browne and Pontifex families.

Several copies of her book 'The Crystal Cabinet' are available at the local libraries.

HEATHSIDE

Avalon, the pleasant residential development designed by Basil White architect from Sopley, near Christchurch, and constructed during the late 1970s, is to be found along Sandbanks Road just before Evening Hill; it stands on the site once occupied by Heathside, a large house, with the entrance lodge Heathside Cottage close to the road. It has been described as house, garden and pleasure ground, and was probably built around 1840.

Reading Freda Neale's recently published 'History of Conifer Park' we know that in 1844 it was owned by Samuel Solly who came from Swinderby in Lincolnshire, and that he also owned the 30 acre Myrtle Farm, which is now part of the Conifer Park Estate. He died in 1847 and his widow Dorothea in 1877.

It seems that the next owner might have been a Colonel Everett, who lived at Heathside with his sister. In her book 'The Crystal Cabinet', Mary Butts from Salterns House wrote 'I loved their home, chiefly for the trees. There was a rough lawn in front of the house, turf so rough that it was purple with orchids in the spring. A set of ilexes, enormous and of great age with one so large it split into three and had to be propped up'. This would probably have been in the early 1900s.

We know that when the London architect John James Joass purchased Flag Farm in 1925 he was already the owner of Heathside and according to Kelly's Directory was still the owner in 1930; with Heathside Cottage occupied by Arthur Painter.

In Pevsner we read that 'Heathside was originally slate-roofed stucco, as was the lodge with its cast-iron colonnade'. He described John Joass as 'an innovating Edwardian classicist, who ran verandahs to both floors extending beyond the house at each end in a delicate white net of tensely drawn pairs of uprights and crossbars. It is in a sort of stripped chinoiserie, Regency plantation house in flavour, without stylistic ornament, and has rich red pantiles'.

Pevsner also mentioned Wayfoong in Crichel Mount Road (now a small cul-de-sac) which Mr Joass designed for his brother Henry Crawford Joass - 'it is a disappointment, a white rectangle under a hipped slate roof, irregularly punctuated by Georgian-shaped windows'.

The author walking along Sandbanks Road
towards Evening Hill - 19.2.78.
On left an estate agent's board announcing the commencement
of the development of Avalon on the site of Heathside.

Kelly's Directory 1939 tells us that James Albert King was then living at Heathside with Arthur Painter still in the lodge; and next door at Coolhurst (now a block of flats) was Major O'Hara Moore. By 1961 the lodge was occupied by R H Rowe, and James A King was still in the house.

In the early 1970s Heathside was demolished (the lodge survived a little longer) and although many were felled, it is believed that a few of the original trees remain.

LILLIPUT HOUSE

A terrace promenade occupying the whole of the south front, croquet lawns, an Italian garden and a brick built racquet court with a Sun Temple were some of the outdoor facilities on offer with Lilliput House when Hankinson and Son, Bournemouth estate agents, handled the auction on Thursday 24th July 1919. Described as an exceedingly attractive and picturesque residence in Lilliput, near Bournemouth, the particulars stated that Lilliput House, set in 12 acres, occupied one of the finest positions in the south of England, overlooking Brownsea Island and Poole Harbour.

We learn that its situation is well above sea level, and prospective purchasers would no doubt have been pleased to find that the sanitation is on modern principles, with the property drained into the public sewer.

Included in the sale were lodges, detached and secondary stabling, a coachman's cottage, glass houses and garden buildings - these included a full span, a small span and a $^3/_4$ span glass house, a range of brick pits, a small lean-to vinery house, potting and tool sheds and a forcing house.

In recent years the locally listed property has been divided into two separate dwellings and the detached stabling converted into a house, whilst the lodge and secondary stabling, which included a coach house, loose box and harness room, are now separate entities; other houses have been built in the grounds.

Dating back to around 1889 Lilliput House was built on part of the Flag Farm Estate, and documents of the time contain the names of The Right Honourable Henry Gerard Baron Alington and The Honourable Humphrey Napier Sturt together with Henry Forde and The Reverend Henry George Watkins. The last named may possibly have been the first owner of the property and it seems that his widow, Marie Heloise Watkins was the vendor in 1919. It is believed that Reverend and Mrs Watkins were the grandparents of the explorer, Gino Watkins, who was tragically killed at a very young age. Other names connected with the property were William Chinchen (1894)-in the 1939 Kelly's a builder W B Chinchen was living in Lilliput Road on the site of Lagado Close; Major James William Garton JP (1939), John Gwynne Crosby in 1950, and in 1961, possibly remembered by some older folk, was John Bruce Trevelyan Thomas, Ophthalmic Surgeon.

'This beautiful residence, in the Elizabethan style of architecture, is well and substantially built of red brick with timbered upper stories and red tiled roof, and is approached by a winding drive bordered on either side by flower beds and graceful pines'. This was the estate agents description of the house at the time of the 1919 auction; there were eleven bedrooms (on two floors) plus three others approached through a baize swing door to the back landing and a housemaid's closet, so presumably these were the servants quarters. There were plenty of ground floor rooms to enjoy - an entrance hall with mosaic floor, lounge hall with polished oak floor and panelled ceiling (off this a butler's room), a music room with a private staircase to the sleeping chamber above, a cosy sitting room, a double drawing room with an Adam ceiling and copper canopies to the stoves at each end, the terrace promenade, a dining room with an 'enriched ceiling', a winter garden with glass dome shaped roof and a billiard room. The Domestic Offices were 'well shut off from the principal portion of the house' and comprised the servants hall, house-keeper's room, butler's pantry, kitchen, scullery, larder, coal cellar and boot room.

It appears that the property was not, in fact, sold at the 1919 auction, but subsequently to an unknown purchaser in September 1920.

Hill Cottage in Minterne Road is believed to have been the secondary stabling for Lilliput House. Mrs Mavis Perrins and her family lived there in the years immediately following WWII - the road was unmade and the large houses of Wentworth, Witley and Minterne Grange still stood. There was a yard at the rear where the carriage was washed, stalls for the horses still existed and the huge hay loft, in which they installed a bathroom. From the windows of Hill Cottage, in the winter time, her two young sons used to watch the gas lamps being lit, one by one, around the harbour wall.

FLAG FARM

On the corner of Shore Road with Brudenell Avenue are now three houses - Threave, Flag Farm House and Gulliver House; they cover the site of an old property with associated outbuildings which was demolished in 1995. Believed to have been late Elizabethan or early Jacobean, Flag Farm was originally called Haven House within the Haven Estate on land which is shown on old maps as North Haven.

In the late 18th and early 19th Centuries it was known as Lilliput Farm. C. Cochrane, in his 'Poole Bay and Purbeck 1660-1920' suggests that the change of name may have had a connection with the then owner, Isaac Gulliver (1745-1822) whose rise to respectability from smuggling to becoming a banker in Wimborne, coincided with a map dated 1805-7 naming it Lilliput Farm. It is marked thus in a Hydrographic Office survey of Poole Harbour dated 1902, but at some stage after that the name was changed again, to Flag Farm, and this is believed to have a link with the Coastguard Station on the cliffs at, what is now known as, Flaghead Chine.

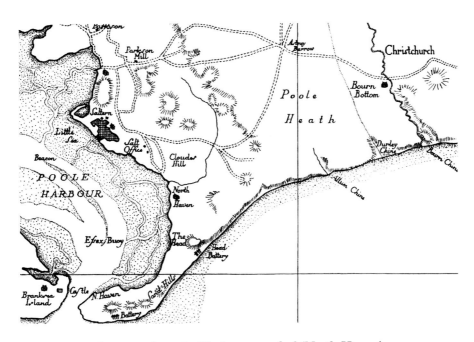

A very early map. The house marked 'North Haven'
is almost certainly Flag Farm.
Courtesy: The Editor, 'Dorset Year Book'.

By 1918 Kelly's Directory tells us that a dairy farmer Arthur Wightman was living at Flag Farm, and it appears that the next owner endeavoured to modernise the building by removing the old staircase, and filling in the basement cellar and creamery.

Although Flag Farm was the oldest property in Parkstone, it was not a listed building and had been greatly altered over the years both inside and out; despite strenuous efforts to prevent its demise, demolition occurred in 1995.

In the 1942/3 Dorset Year Book Mr H P Smith, the Poole historian who re-discovered Scaplens Court in 1923, wrote a long description of Flag Farm and its owners, from which we learn that the then occupant, a Mrs Cox, uncovered some of the ancient features. The original walls were built with two feet thick Purbeck stone and some had later been faced with brickwork. Old fireplaces were found behind the modern ones and two complete tree trunks were revealed in the hall which stretched across the ceiling as beams. The steps leading to the creamery were also discovered below the passage floor. The bakehouse at the entrance to the property contained a capacious oven sufficient for a batch of three dozen loaves, so perhaps the baking was done for all the farm labourers. As well as a Victorian kitchen range in the same building, two earlier fireplaces were discovered together with fragments of hand-made wine glasses and pretty pieces of china. A thick deposit of oyster shells were found in the garden, and a number of Georgian coins which were presented to Poole Museum.

Mandy Loader, whose aunt Mrs Phyllis Edwards lived at Flag Farm for over 20 years in more recent times, recalls an orchard in the garden and the thick stone walls of the house. She spoke of tales of a tunnel to Brownsea Island, and a top-hatted ghost playing a violin!

The Haven Estate extended to the seashore (The Head) and back along Lilliput Road, which is known to have been an old trackway made up in the 1920s and included 'the ford and passage where the waggons pass'. The bank at the rear of the bungalows in Lagado Close is believed to be the 'Elizabethan boundary that separated the Haven Farm Estate on Evening Hill from the copperas workings along Lilliput Road' - a photograph of this was included in C Cochrane's 'Poole Bay and Purbeck 300 BC -AD 1600'. Parcels of land on the estate were marked as Compton Acre, Bee Garden, Broadshard, Bean Garden and Ferney Plot.

A document dated 1617 records the sale of Haven House with its lands to Nicholas Meade of Barkham in Berkshire, from the estate of the Earl of Huntingdon. It was the Huntingdon family who had acquired the Canford Estates from the Mountjoys in 1570 and who had been so active in exploiting the copperas mines at Parkstone and Brownsea. The property then passed to Mr Meade's granddaughter Elizabeth, wife of John Morris, who appear to have shared it with Haviland Hiley and his wife Mary.

The Cload family were the next owners of the Haven Estate, who held it for over 100 years. Starting with Captain Thomas Cload, a wealthy mariner, it passed to his son George and thence to his son Thomas. What is now Evening Hill has in the past been marked on maps as Oakman's Hill (1748), Cloude's Hill (1765), Cload's Hill and Lilliput Hill Road (1937).

In 1768 or 1799 Charles Sturt, who also owned Moor Crichel and Brownsea Island, acquired the Haven Estate from the executors of Thomas Cload (Samuel Clark of Poole and Peregrine Baker the younger, yeoman of Parkstone). No further information regarding subsequent owners is available until 1925.

Flag Farm was sold by The Right Honourable Napier George Henry Baron Alington and The Right Honourable Arthur Robert Baron Hillingdon to John James Joass and his wife Mary

Widdicombe Joass on 11th September 1925, and the Conveyance states: 'No house already erected or to be erected on the premises shall be used for the purpose of any trade or business except that of a Farmer, Market Gardener or boarding or lodging house keeper. No portion of the land shall be used as an advertisement station. The purchasers shall not bake or burn any bricks pipes earth or clay on the premises'. There were restrictions on the height of trees with reference to sea views and the purchasers were to erect good substantial cleft oak fencing not exceeding five feet in height.

Flag Farm on left at the junction of Shore Road with Brudenell Avenue.
The name of the house on the right is unknown.
Courtesy: Mrs Jane Attia.

J J Joass was a London architect (Belcher and Joass) who, it seems already had a seaside home in the area - Heathside on Sandbanks Road (now Avalon); and it was a maid from Heathside, E Sturney, who witnessed the signature of Mrs N W Joass on the Conveyance.

Auction Particulars from Rumsey and Rumsey dated September 1961 indicate that Flag Farm then had five bedrooms and three reception rooms, and within the three-quarters of an acre plot was a three room cottage. Outline planning permission existed to convert the property into two self-contained flats and to sever a 'valuable residential building plot'; Brudenell Avenue and Brudenell Road were unmade and unadopted at the time.

LEWIS-MANNING

The Lewis-Manning Hospice Day Centre is to be found in Crichel Mount Road. Run as an independent charity with funds raised by voluntary donations, it is a day centre for cancer patients requiring palliative, or hospice, care. The aim is to provide facilities for helping and supporting people (and their families) living with cancer, to alleviate suffering and to improve the quality of their lives. The specialist care covers a wide range of physical, mental, spiritual and social help within a pleasant environment, and the spacious grounds overlooking Poole Harbour provide a peaceful setting.

Once called 'Evening Hill' the property, from the 1960s, was in the ownership of Mr R H Lewis-Manning, a local solicitor, and his wife Marjorie. After his death from cancer, Mrs Lewis-Manning devoted her time and energy to raising money for treatment of the disease. She launched the Body Scanner Appeal and set up the Poole Hospital Cancer Treatment Trust; a sum in excess of four and a half million pounds was raised.

When Mrs Lewis-Manning died in 1987 she left her home and estate to be used as a hospice. A recent extension, opened by Her Grace The Duchess of Norfolk CBE, further improved the range of facilities available, and the Lewis-Manning Hospice Day Care Centre is always pleased to receive donations, and offers of voluntary help.

On the opposite side of the road a new house is currently being constructed on the site of Minterne Cottage. This is believed to have been the lodge for Minterne Grange (now flats); in 1939 Mr C P Charles was in residence at The Grange and Sidney William Nicholls in the lodge. At one time the property was used as a stable and hay loft, but in 1950 was converted into a private home, and in 1983 was for sale as a luxurious cottage. It was demolished in 1998.

TINKERS REVEL

Further up the road is locally listed Tinkers Revel, being described as 'a quaint rustic house style with strong medieval references in its leaded windows and timber framing'. Built in 1936 it includes some materials from Hampreston Manor House, and the design is reputed to be a replica of the Hollywood home of a film star of that era - Deanna Durbin.

LANDFALL

Also in Crichel Mount Road is the only Grade II listed building in Lilliput - dating from 1938/9 Landfall was designed by the architect Oliver Hill, who greatly admired the work of Sir Edward Lutyens.

Pevsner described it thus. 'Announced by a curving white wall, this is a delicious design, set in a pine forest, with a stark counterpoint of transparency and foliage. The solid-walled entrance front, its curving staircase bay pierced by portholes, is the backcloth for the almost wholly glazed garden side, which has continuous balconies on tubular steel posts connected by an elegant spiral stairway of concrete at one corner. Inside, the three main living rooms can be thrown into one, a sinuous timber staircase leading to the sun room on the roof'.

The site was purchased from Lord Alington in 1937 by Mr and Mrs Shaw Ashton, who were living in Canford Cliffs at the time. In their early 20s, they both took an interest in design and talked to several famous architects before choosing Oliver Hill.

Taking an active part in the original design, the modifications and subsequent progress of the building work, Dudley Shaw Ashton made a film of the whole project, and entering it in a National Amateur film competition, won first prize. This launched him into his professional career as a film director; many of his films were commissioned by the Arts Council and included the work of Henry Moore, that of Barbara Hepworth and the building of Coventry Cathedral by Sir Basil Spence. Several are now to be found in the National Film Archives.

The film of the construction of Landfall proved to be very useful at a later date. About a year after Mr and Mrs Shaw Ashton had moved in, the wooden floor in the lounge began to lift. It was only when the builder was shown the film did he agree that the damp proof course over the concrete had *not* been laid and he was forced to agree to lay the damp proof course and re-lay the floor!

Oliver Hill was a man with many interests - and eccentricities - for the film of the building work show him carrying a monkey on his shoulder. He also enjoyed sunbathing and there are stories about the difficulties this produced for him.

'Landfall' Courtesy: John Liddell

Mr and Mrs Shaw Ashton commissioned furniture by Betty Joel; the original cedar fitments in the lounge and the 'Ashton' dining table and chairs have been retained together with paintings and murals. The present owners have added further interesting furniture and decorative pieces made by Dorset craftsmen. The back of the downstairs cloakroom door was used as the visitors book by Mr and Mrs Ashton who asked their guests, famous and otherwise, to sign their names. Those still visible include Henry Moore and Jacquetta Hawkes.

Oliver Hill was a Fellow of the Institute of Landscape Architects and had collaborated with Gertrude Jekyll on various garden designs; and created three vistas for the garden at Landfall. As a foil to the starkness of the lines of the house, the naturalness of the wooded area was retained and, since flowers upset Dudley Ashton's asthma, the garden was planted with rhododendrons. The severe gales of recent years caused many of the original pines to fall and the garden now has a more open aspect with camellias and azaleas in a woodland setting. An air-raid shelter, with electric light and bunks, was built under the terrace just after the house was completed and the Ashton family spent many nights there during WWII (1939-1945).

An exhibition of Oliver Hill's work took place in 1989 at the Royal Institute of British Architects and since then there has been an increased interest in houses of this style and period.

Landfall was the home of Mr and Mrs Shaw Ashton and their two sons for 43 years; when they moved out in 1980 the property was sold to Mr and Mrs Keeling who lived there five years. Planning applications were refused for a mansard roof and to separate a plot, and in 1981 Landfall became a Grade II Listed Building.

The present owners enjoy living in the house and are conscious of the need to preserve this fine example of 1930s architecture and interior design; documents and films relating to the history of Landfall have been carefully collated and stored. The archives of The Tate Gallery in St Ives, Cornwall now contain Dudley Shaw Ashton's correspondence with reference to Barbara Hepworth.

GRAY RIGG

The stables and squash court at Gray Rigg (called Crichel Place at one time) are locally listed, but the house itself is not. Described as a rambling, picturesque late Victorian house of red brick with stone decoration in the Gothic style, it was built in 1895 or 1897 as a 'gentleman's residence'. The seven and a half acres which reached down to Bingham Avenue included 'a lovely tropical garden, tennis court and croquet green, lily pond and lawns, beautiful terraces with climbing roses and wisteria and a lovely mimosa tree'. At the time there were views over Parkstone Golf Course and across to Brownsea Island.

It is known that Mr Harold Soames bought the property in 1908 and lived there with his wife Katharine and daughters Auriol and Olave for a number of years before Mr and Mrs Kenneth Tyrer became the owners - their three daughters attended Sandecotes School (now Uplands). In the late 1920s the house was sold to Mr Graham Wright together with Fellside Cottages in Bingham Avenue, and according to Kelly's Directories Mr William Beaufort Clayton lived there in 1939 and Mr S E N Whitelock in 1961.

Fellside Cottages in Bingham Avenue, one of which was the childhood home of Mrs Margaret Fellows in the early 1900s. Courtesy: Mr John Tucker

It was from her home at Gray Rigg that Olave St Clair Soames, later Lady Baden-Powell GBE, set forth to marry Sir Robert Baden-Powell (founder of the Boy Scout Movement) in October 1912 at St Peter's Church in Ashley Cross. Initially, the Church of the Holy Angels was chosen for the ceremony but as public interest grew and threatened to overwhelm the occasion, the bride and groom opted for a small family service elsewhere.

The Soames family originated in Chesterfield, and after Mr Soames sold his brewing business there they lived in many different houses in various parts of the country. On coming to Gray Rigg Mrs Soames declared that 'Lilliput was the desired compromise between town and country without being aggressively suburban'. Lady Baden-Powell herself called the house 'Grig'.

On 15th May 1963 Lady Baden-Powell, who was a Freeman of the Borough of Poole, officially opened Brownsea Island for the National Trust, and on that same day took the opportunity of driving round to look at Gray Rigg. Unfortunately, it seems that the area had changed so much that she hardly recognised it.

During the years that Mr and Mrs Soames lived at the house, Mr Thomas Tucker was the head gardener and he lived in one of the Fellside Cottages in Bingham Avenue, whilst the chauffeur Mr Puddle (previously the coachman) lived in the other cottage. During WWI (1914-1918) Mr Tucker worked at Poole Iron Foundry from 6.00 am to 5.00 pm and did his best to look after the greenhouses and gardens at Gray Rigg in his spare time.

He had six surviving children - two sons and four daughters and the youngest daughter Margaret kept a diary of her early years. Born in Fellside Cottages around 1908 she was christened at the Church of the Holy Angels, attended the church school in Lilliput Road and went on to St Peter's School in Ashley Cross. One of her sisters, Flo, was under housemaid to the Soames family at Gray Rigg, and later Margaret herself went as a kitchenmaid there in the days of Mr and Mrs Tyrer. Her memories of the area and life in general were quite remarkable and I am indebted to her two surviving nephews, Mr John Tucker and Mr Tony Baker, for permission to use her reminiscences.

Mr Tucker himself was christened at the Church of the Holy Angels and as a young lad during the years of WWII (1939-1945) was a delivery boy in the Canford Cliffs and Lilliput area. He recalls the residence of Lord Lyle in Nairn Road, the tin hut of the Working Men's Club in Lilliput Road, the Command Post at the bottom of Brudenell Avenue (concrete still there) and the Auxiliary Fire Station where now stands a small block of flats, The Clock, in Lilliput Square. Milk for the area used to be supplied from Flag Farm and it is said the round always ended up at The Beehive. There is a story that one day, for whatever reason, the vicar of St Mary's on Brownsea, did the round, and the horse quite naturally took him into The Beehive!

It was probably after the end of WWI that Margaret Tucker went to work for Mr and Mrs Tyrer as kitchenmaid at Gray Rigg, her wage being £18.00 a year. Before she commenced her duties three uniform dresses had to be made, unbleached linen sewn into aprons with bibs and coarse waist aprons and new black stockings bought, together with flat shoes. These were packed into an old tin trunk, put on a wheelbarrow and taken by her father to the big house.

Margaret shared a bedroom with the under housemaid - it had been Lady Baden-Powell's schoolroom and had 'wonderful views from the big windows right across Poole Harbour'. She was introduced to the other staff - Miss Bowden cook-housekeeper, Frances the parlour maid,

Mrs Grant head housemaid, Ada sewing and schoolroom maid and Kathleen under housemaid. Mr Harvey the butler lived in a cottage at the back of the stables.

Lilliput Road - John Tucker and Tony Baker
with an older relative - late 1920s.
Courtesy: Mr John Tucker

Her duties included being up at 6.00 am to clean the kitchen range, dust and sweep the servants hall and lay the table for staff breakfast, scrub the front door step and polish the entrance hall floor. After taking tea up to the cook, Margaret was able to enjoy her own early morning tea and biscuits. She dealt with the staff washing up and was allowed to do only the plates from the dining room (the parlourmaid was entrusted with the silver and the best china). Coal scuttles had to be filled, knives cleaned 'in the boot hall with a Spong machine'; and whilst sweeping the back door step Margaret would look around in the hope of seeing her father (head gardener) in the distance.

From Margaret's description of her working life it seems that conditions were favourable - plenty of good food, time off for holidays, staff outings to the pantomime at the Theatre Royal in Bournemouth and visits to agricultural and horse shows.

A number of dogs lived at Gray Rigg and Margaret was in charge of their food, preparing the meat on a small stove in the scullery - Scamp the collie, Spot the black and tan terrier, Jimmy the whippet and another little rough black and tan terrier. Each Christmas, Don the black retriever was chosen to take a £1. note to Margaret as thanks for feeding him and his pals through the year. The Tyrer family were all keen horse riders and the five hunters in the stables were cared for by Mr Read.

When the family returned to Chester, Margaret went with them for several years before taking a similar post in London; later returning to this area as cook to the Eysoldt family at Imbrecourt in Haven Road (the name of this house is preserved in a cul-de-sac off Nairn Road). Margaret married in 1941 and settled in Parkstone.

The then Margaret Tucker, kitchenmaid at Gray Rigg,
with Mr Harvey, the butler. 1920s.
Courtesy: Mr John Tucker

BINGHAM AVENUE

We learn from her reminiscences that Lilliput Road was not made up until the 1920s, and she described Lilliput as 'a lovely village almost built in a circle, and so many intellectual and interesting people living there'. Margaret wrote of the people residing in Bingham Avenue - from Fellside Cottages there was the vicarage, Miss Parson's guest house and then Mr N G Abraham, who helped the war effort by making 'important small parts' in his garden workshop and employed several men from the village; next came a widow with two young children, who eventually married the vicar from the Church of the Holy Angels, Reverend St Lo Auber, Miss Haskell's private boarding school and at Tal-an-Vean Colonel T and Mrs Maud Diver - she was a prolific novelist writing about military life in India and the NorthWest Frontier as well as 'Speed the Plough' in 1923 and 'Death of Felicity Taverner' in 1932. Further along were a Mr and Mrs Holman - 'he always looked stern and his wife was very stately', and then Mr and Mrs Pullman, who were remembered because they owned a car (unusual then) and had a wall mounted VR letterbox by their gate.

The village policeman lived opposite Margaret's home and next door was a naval man with his wife and family, who kept poultry. Further down was 'a lovely house and grounds and lodge' belonging to Mr and Mrs Mauleverer, this was Mount Grace. I believe the house still stands but is no longer called by that name; part of the grounds now contain Mount Grace Drive. This was developed after WWII and an estate agent's brochure 'Homes in Bournemouth Districts' states 'Mount Grace Estate - Mr Rodd's New Houses, 2 reception, 4 bed, one bath, one garage at £2,500.00.'

It appears that in Margaret's childhood there was a path across the Luscombe Valley from Bingham Avenue since she writes of 'a lovely walk which led to fields which in spring were gay with bluebells and the occasional wild orchid'; the fields led to barns and cowsheds and across the road, which is now Brudenell Avenue, lay a picturesque farmhouse - Flag Farm. From here milk was delivered in the area - jugs were left out on door steps to be filled and in summer the churn was covered with white muslin. Apparently there was a gate across Bingham Avenue and this was closed for one day a year, presumably to remind the public that it was then a private road.

Returning to Lilliput Road, Margaret mentions the old Post Office and general stores; a great attraction to the children was the 'Poll Parrot' which in summer was on a stand in the garden and was a real chatter-box. During the winter 'Poll' was indoors at the back of the shop and whenever a customer entered, would call out 'shop'. The parrot was also able to say clearly the names of the owner and his family.

Postcard c 1930. Clockwise from top left - Poole Harbour from Sandbanks;
Entrance to Poole Harbour; Poole Harbour from Evening Hill; The Cliff Walk.
Courtesy: Lilliput W I

ACKNOWLEDGEMENTS

I am grateful to the following people for providing me with information, and thank them for their help. Please forgive me if I have forgotten anyone.

Mrs Grace Aldridge, Mrs Jane Attia, Mr Tony Baker, Mrs Jean Barnes, Mrs Mary Burden, Mrs Beryl Cotton, Mr Gordon Cousins, Mrs Dolly Dale, Mr T R M Denley, Mr Cecil Edney, Mr H C W Geach, Miss Barbara Graves, Colonel A Heron, Mr Basil Hodder, Mr L C Jenkins, Mr K O Karme, Wing Cdr (Rtd) R W Kemsley, Mr G E Lanning (Editor Dorset Year Book), Ms Mandy Loader, Mr Philip Okey, Mrs D M Parish, Mrs Mavis Perrins, Mr Ken Pizey, Poole Reference Library, Local Studies Collection of Poole Museum Service, Mr John N J Smith, Mrs Sheena Tree, Mr John Tucker, Dr and Mrs C E Upton, Mr Len Webster Archivist at Eldridge Pope, Dr J D Wheatcroft.

BIBLIOGRAPHY

Autobiography of Olave, Lady Baden-Powell GBE
as told to Mary Drewery *Window On My Heart 1973*

Butts, Mary *The Crystal Cabinet 1937*

Cochrane, C *Poole Bay and Purbeck Volume I 1970 and Volume II 1971*

Dawson, Leslie *Wings Over Dorset 1983*

Heron, Alan *History of Lilliput Sailing Club 1997*

Jenkins, L C *History of Parkstone Golf Club 1987*

Lees, L G L and Geach, H C W *History of East Dorset Sailing Club 1975*

Mills, A D *Place Names of Dorset 1986*

Neale, Freda D *A History of Conifer Park 1999*

Pevsner, Nikolaus and Newman, John *The Buildings of England 1972 - Dorset*

Popplewell, Lawrence *High Horse Manger 1987*

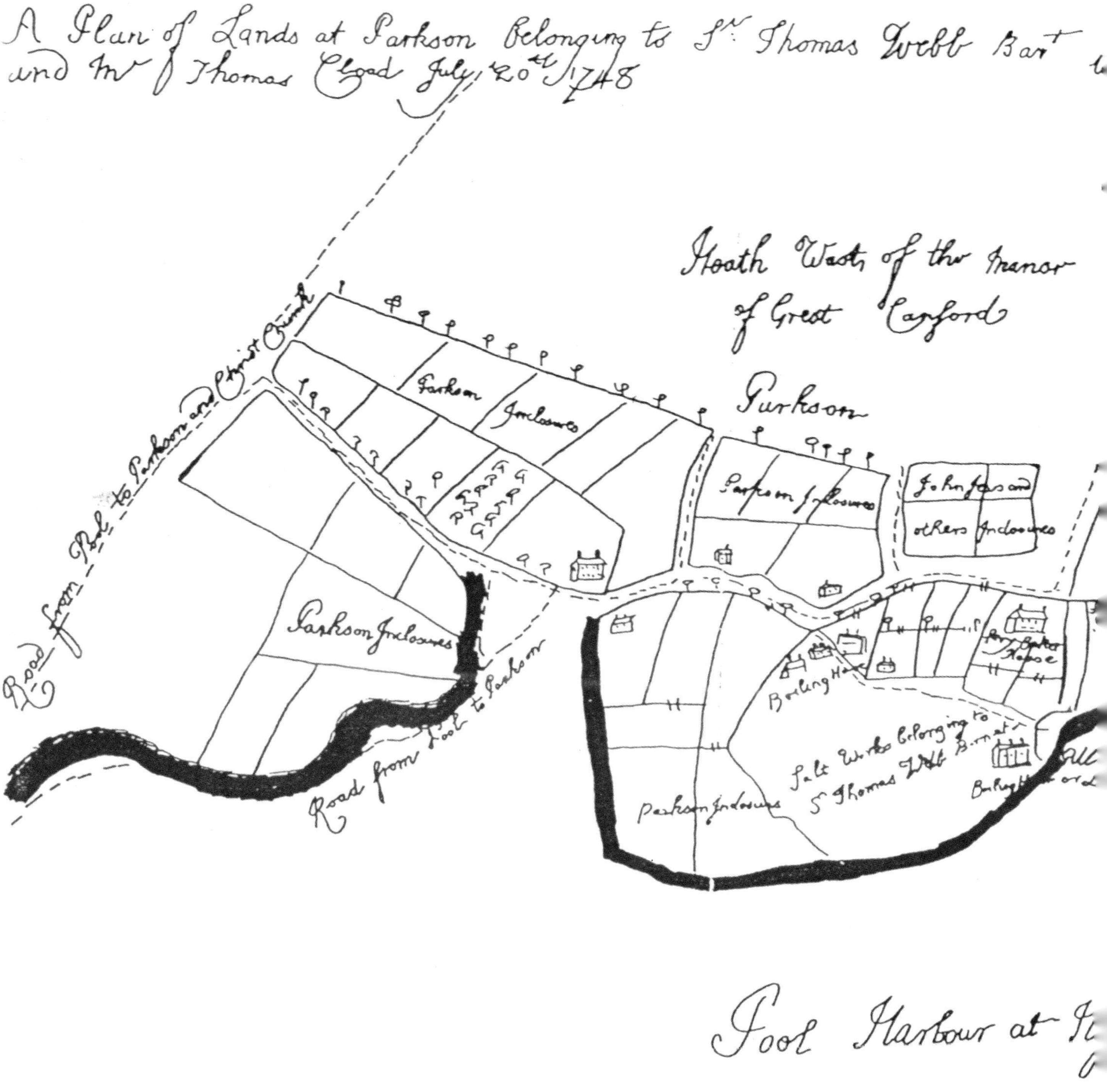

A Plan of Lands at Parkson belonging to Sr. Thomas Webb Bart
and Mr. Thomas Cload July 20th 1748

Heath Waste of the Manor
of Great Canford

Parkson

Parkson Inclosures

Parkson Inclosures

John Toms and
others Inclosures

Road from Pool to Parkson and Christ Church

Parkson Inclosures

Road from Pool to Parkson

Boiling Ho.

Salt House

Salt Works belonging to
Sr. Thomas Webb Bart.

Parkson Inclosures

Boiling House

Pool Harbour at